21ST CENTURY

21ST CENTURY

America's New Declaration of Independence

Wayne Guinn

WINEPRESS WP PUBLISHING

ISBN 1-57921-165-8
Library of Congress Catalog Card Number: 98-88802

Dedication

There are so many people in my life whom I desire to thank for their help and encouragement, that I would be afraid to list them for fear of forgetting someone. Let me offer a summary to these many friends and loved ones.

To my wife and children for their inspiration, love, and encouragement to complete this book, I offer my thanks. To the latest edition to the Guinn family—our first grandchild—I am thankful for the inspiration to see that America needs to change for this, a new generation of Americans. I pray I will be found faithful to uphold and share the principles of this book for her and for her generation.

To those in our armed services—past and present—my undying remembrance and gratitude for their selfless acts of courage and their commitment to the ideals and preservation of our freedom, without which there would be no America today.

To my friends, who have listened to me share the dream of this book, and who supported me with their kind words, many readings, and help in editing and researching this book. Their caring support and stories have been unwavering.

To my father and his mother (my grandmother), who provided a life of caring and inspiration, there are not enough words to say thanks. I know the examples of their lives have inspired many, not the least of whom has been me.

As you may sense, this list could go on forever, but I want to add one last thanks. To all of you who will pick up the challenge by purchasing this book and by sharing and supporting the ideas expressed in it, I want to offer my thanks on behalf of my family and future generations of Americans. My prayer is that together we might set an example that will cause others to remember the twenty-first century as the dawn of a new day in America. To these I give my deepest, heartfelt thanks! May God truly bless America, home of some of the most caring, most brave, and most free people on this planet. May the light of your example still shine today!

Contents

SECTION III: RETAKING OUR AMERICA

Introduction

. . . You will lend to many nations but will borrow from none. The Lord will make you the head, not the tail. If you pay attention to the commands of the Lord your God that I give you this day and carefully follow them, you will always be at the top, never at the bottom. (Deut. 28:12–13)

At the time of the writing of this book in 1998, America's national debt stands somewhere between five and six trillion dollars, with interest compounding daily. Most of us recognize that to be a staggering amount, but I wonder if we even begin to comprehend just how overwhelming it actually is.

In 1986, when the national debt reached $2 trillion, one economist painted a graphic picture to help us visualize the enormity of that debt. He estimated that if the $2 trillion were split into one-thousand dollar bills and stacked one on top of the other, the stack would reach a height of about 135 miles. But with the current national debt at almost three times that amount, we're now talking about a 400-mile-high sky-scraper! As a citizen and a taxpayer, does that frighten you? It should! And as America continues with business as usual, how long can this ever-increasing monolith sustain itself before it topples over and comes crashing down on all of us? Not long, I would think. And most financial experts, as well as the politicians primarily responsible for sustaining and feeding this growing albatross, agree. However, to date, no one has come up with a viable solution.

In fact, at this point, the closest thing we have to a proposed solution is one of former Republican Representative Mark Neumann from Wisconsin. According to *U.S. News*, Neumann's proposal was favorably received by many within his party, including former Speaker of the House Newt Gingrich, who worked hard to promote the idea to other conservative activists. Even former presidential candidate, Ross Perot, seems to like the idea. He has thrown his support behind the proposal and considered plugging it on television infomercials. But not everyone is favorably impressed with Neumann's brainchild. Several liberal, as well as conservative, economists have labeled his idea as "fundamentally dumb," despite its tremendous political appeal.

So just what was Neumann's proposal, and how did he come up with it? Mark Neumann, a former math teacher who made his fortune as a homebuilder, based his proposal on the premise that what worked for him as a small businessman, would also work for the federal government.

Basically, Neumann suggested that government should not be satisfied with balancing the budget, but rather it should take it a step further and find ways to pay off its national debt. When revenue and spending trends lend themselves to balancing the budget, the government should endeavor to sustain these trends, applying surpluses to the national debt until it is dissolved. Neumann's plan required that "the federal budget run surpluses every year by capping overall spending at 1 percent less than the amount of revenue collected." One-third of this surplus cash is allocated "to pay for tax cuts, a third to road-building and other projects, and a third to pay off the debt."[1] For many, particularly those fearful of more and bigger government, the idea is quite appealing—especially when you consider Neumann's claims that America would be debt-free in approximately twenty-five years.

Economists, however, are fearful of chronic surpluses, claiming they can be "almost as threatening as chronic debt, since they take some purchasing power out of an economy and can cause recession. . . . Virtually no academic economist endorses the payoff idea."[2] And some within Neumann's Republican Party would rather concentrate more on cutting taxes than cutting spending. Jack Kemp is against the proposal, as is the *Wall Street Journal*, which has labeled it "invincible ignorance."

But even with its vocal critics and possible downside, Neumann's proposal seems to be the "only game in town," which of course, explains its widespread appeal. However, I believe there is another very viable alternative, which I will present in this book. I will do that by first retracing the foundation of values in our American culture and then contrasting those values with the values in today's culture, which I believe, have led to our burgeoning mountain of debt. When we realize where we have come from in our American heritage, and then compare that to today's values, we will see the obvious need to make changes that, when implemented, will lead Americans to agree on a plan to end our cycle of debt.

In making these changes and allowing our nation to reinstate parts of our American heritage, we can convert our existing national obligations and budgeted expenses in such a way as to ensure ongoing provision for America's healthcare and retirement needs. This will allow citizens to regain their lost dreams, while at the same time, enable our nation to eliminate our national debt within our lifetime.

If we don't make these changes, America will continue the slide it began in the 1940s, down a slippery slope into the ever-widening abyss of national debt, which threatens to swallow up the hopes and dreams of future Americans. As Proverbs 22:7 so aptly warns us, ". . . the borrower is servant to the lender." Our nation cannot remain strong and secure while burdened with such a huge debt. This is a growing problem for many reasons, all of which are significant beyond even the potential for national disgrace and bankruptcy. This economic situation is robbing American families of small-business opportunities; first-time home buyers of the opportunity for a new home; American businesses of the opportunity to finance expansion and growth; and America itself of the opportunity to finance the rebuilding of needed public infrastructures, such as roads, transportation, and bridges.

I am proposing a plan, which, if followed, can set a pattern for turning this destructive tidal wave of debt into a tool that can provide for new growth, economic opportunity, and even hope for those who are less fortunate in our society. Some of the details of this plan will be revealed in this book. Let me share a story, often used as a sermon illustration by a pastor friend of mine; it illustrates a principle that relates to dealing with reducing the national debt and other problems that face our country.

It seems a farmer was working in his field, plowing and preparing his soil for planting. He was a poor farmer who had one plow and one mule to pull the plow. This farmer and mule had spent many years together, preparing for sea-

son after season of crops. On this particular occasion, the
farmer went back to the barn to gather some tools to repair
the plow harness. He decided to set the mule free of the
harness and plow so it could roam in the field while he was
gone. As the mule wandered in the field, it stumbled into
an old abandoned well that, with time, had grown over with
weeds. The mule lay at the bottom of this deep pit, dazed,
but only slightly hurt. Yet it was seemingly helpless because
it had fallen so far down the abandoned shaft.

Soon the farmer returned to the field. Noticing that
the mule was nowhere in sight, he began to call and look
for the animal. In one corner of the field, he soon heard a
faint snorting sound. Upon further investigation, he saw
the weed covering disturbed and found his longtime friend,
captured and hurt, down at the bottom of the abandoned
well shaft.

The farmer sat there disturbed and frustrated for several
minutes, talking to the old mule as if he hoped the mule
could tell him some way to solve their problem. Finally, real-
izing he could not get the mule out without causing greater
pain and harm to the animal, as well as possibly falling into
the hole himself, the farmer came up with a plan.

He decided that since there was no way to save his mule,
he would be merciful and bury him where he lay, using
mounds of stone and dirt nearby. Not wanting to see the
mule suffer any further, he began moving dirt into the hole.
Load after load he hauled and dumped. After each load was
dumped into the shaft, the farmer heard the snorting of the
mule grow louder and louder down below. Assuming the
mule was struggling, and it was soon to be overcome by the
suffocating dirt, the farmer worked faster to move the dirt
into the hole.

Many loads later, the farmer returned with yet another load when something caught his eye. For a split second, he thought he saw the mule's head bob up out of the opening of the old well! Telling himself it was only an illusion, the tired farmer dumped in this load of dirt and knowing that the sun would soon set, he went back for what he thought should be the last load. Again, he heard the snorting sound and could see dirt rising out of the opening of the well. Feeling compassion for the mule, the farmer hastened back for the final load, which he intended to use to completely fill in the well.

When he reached the opening, he paused and looked down to bid the mule a final farewell. To the farmer's amazement, there stood the mule, just a couple of feet from the surface of the old well! The farmer finally realized that while he was dumping in dirt to bury the mule, the animal was stomping, snorting, and packing down the dirt. With every load, the mule had packed another layer under his feet, moving him closer and closer to the top of the well. The farmer was amazed and overwhelmed. What he thought would bury the mule, was the very thing the animal used to save his life. Each load dumped in, brought the mule that much closer to the top of that old well. In amazement, the farmer dumped in the final load of dirt, then watched as his weary friend stepped out onto solid ground.

Just as the well brought the mule's life into jeopardy, the national debt and other problems within our country are creating a similar pit, ready to swallow up the dreams and futures of many American generations. However, like the example of the mule, I believe the very things that could bring about the death of many Americans' dreams, can be turned into a tool to bring America and its next generations out onto solid economic ground. This very debt, which could drag us all down in international disgrace and financial slavery, can become a tool that we can forge into building our future.

I believe that to understand what has brought America to the precipice of this financial disaster, we must also understand that is only one symptom of a larger problem, which has slowly engulfed, and now permeates, America as a nation. To show this, this book will give examples of some of our early American heroes so we can see what once made our nation great. Next, it will anger you as you see how people and institutions have disassembled the principles that made America great. Lastly, this book will attempt to outline answers to today's major issues and will challenge every American to become a part of what could be the greatest declaration signed by Americans in the over two hundred years of our nation's existence.

You are at the point of no return and on the precipice of a new millennium. You can make a difference in our America today! This book seeks to help us all begin a course of action to save our nation from financial and moral disaster, while restoring an America based on the principles upon which it was founded and for which many Americans have given their lives. The answer must begin with each of us— right here, right now, today.

Rediscovering
Our Roots

CHAPTER 1

THE REAL FOUNDATION OF AMERICA

. . . The hour has come for you to wake up from your slumber. . . . (Rom. 13:11)

The fact that America had *two* Great Awakenings can be viewed from two different perspectives.

1. It was good news because our ancestors were blessed with two God-inspired revivals.
2. It was bad news because the effects of the first social awakening wore off so quickly, a second was needed just one-half century later.

Whether you choose to see the glass as half full, or half empty, the fact remains that many of the most significant events in the founding of this nation took place during those five to six decades between the two Great Awakenings.

Who Was Sleeping, and What's a Great Awakening?

We baby boomers—and those who preceded us—learned in school about the Pilgrims' arrival in the New World in search of religious freedom. They were fleeing a country dominated by a state church that had grown cold and was intolerant of their biblical piety and open worship.

But not all those Europeans who arrived at America's eastern seaboard during the seventeenth century came for spiritual reasons. Many, such as the Virginia Company in Virginia, and the Royal Colonies, established in New York and New Hampshire, came primarily in search of economic gain. From the beginning, America's founders brought a mixture of religious and worldly goals and aspirations. At times, "the glass" would seem near to overflowing; at other times, nearly dry.

Although, in the late seventeenth and early eighteenth centuries, atheism was a far-off concept, unimaginable to probably all Americans, the rationalism of the Enlightenment sweeping through Europe was beginning to influence this country. Many Americans liked the idea of an uninvolved God, who had created everything, then established for Himself a hands-off policy, allowing each individual to be the master of his own fate (and society, as the sum of individual choices, to determine its collective fate).

But God raised up the likes of William Tennent, Johnathan Edwards, Gilbert Tennent, Daniel Marshall, Eleazer Wheelock, and George Whitfield, along with many others, to awaken the young country from its spiritual slumber and to challenge it with the needs and possibilities that lay ahead.

Even today, many who know little or nothing about America's Great Awakenings have heard the name Johnathan Edwards. He is most often associated with one short sermon he gave in Enfield in 1741, titled "Sinners in the Hands of an Angry God." But Edwards, a Puritan, was not normally given to emotional, fire-and-brimstone messages. Contrary to the emphasis on morality over faith, which was becoming increasingly popular, Edwards emphasized justification by faith and, in 1734, gave a series of sermons on "Justification by Faith Alone."

Although George Whitfield and Gilbert Tennent drew huge crowds to their fiery sermons and often had mass conversions of convicted sinners, Edwards, perhaps more than anyone else, was God's chief instrument in awakening the people of the young British-American colonies to their need for deep spiritual changes in their lives. Clearly, people were looking for change in their own personal lives and in the governmental affairs of colonial America.

In meeting the needs of the people, there were clear themes to which America rallied and to which revivalists of this time brought vividly to life. I believe we can summarize the themes of the messages, and their impact on the colonists, into the seven basic principles I have listed below

1. To perform hard work as a consistent lifestyle.
2. To develop a thrifty lifestyle and to value the resources of this new land.
3. To develop a sober lifestyle, free from the public drunkenness and brawling, which had become common in Europe and was beginning to reach across the Atlantic to the colonies.
4. To develop an emphasis on the equality of all people before God and with respect to one another.
5. To practice, as a duty, acts of doing good works for the less fortunate in society
6. To emphasize religious pluralism—respect for all denominations of religious belief.
7. To make a commitment to maintain personal standards of morality.

They Lived It

No one better exemplified the principles of hard work, soberness, and personal morality than Johnathan Edwards. Edwards began his studies of Latin when he was just six years old. By the time he entered Yale College (as it was called then) at the age of thirteen, he had a working knowledge of, and fluency in, Latin, Greek, and Hebrew. He graduated at the head of his class when he was just seventeen and began his preaching ministry in New York City at the tender age of nineteen.

There is no room for doubt that Johnathan Edwards was gifted with a brilliant mind. But he bolstered his gift with self-discipline and hard work. He was a prolific thinker and a prolific writer. He almost always had a pen in hand, and he committed his thoughts to writing. Among those many writings were his "Resolutions." There were seventy resolutions, and they were his personal rules of self-discipline—he lived by them. He read them back to himself once each week for his entire life. Here are a few of them:

- Resolved to do whatever I think to be my duty and most for the good and advantage of mankind in general. Resolved to do this, whatever difficulties I meet with, how many and how great so ever.
- Resolved, never to do any manner of thing, whether in soul or body, less or more, but what tends to the glory of God; nor be, nor suffer it, if I can avoid it.
- Resolved to live with all my might, while I do live.
- Resolved, never to do anything out of revenge.

If Johnathan Edwards was the personification of the principles of hard work, soberness, and personal morality, Roger Williams, who preceded Edwards by a century, epitomized all those principles, plus thriftiness, equality, good works for the less fortunate, and religious pluralism—all of the seven principles. The life of Roger Williams stands as a living monument to the principles that made America a great nation.

Because of his unwavering stands for the rights of Indians and against a state church and "forced conversions," Williams was not welcomed in many established New England churches. As a consequence, he established a settlement on the banks of the Seekonk River on a tract of land he bought from his Indian friends. He declared that because of the many "Providences of the Most Holy and Only Wise, I called [my settlement] Providence." That settlement is now known as Providence, Rhode Island. Under Williams' leadership, it would become a haven of peace between Indians and white settlers, as well as a refuge for Quakers, Jews, and others who were fleeing religious or political persecution.

More than 130 years before Americans would find it necessary to declare their independence from an oppressive monarch, Williams wrote these almost prophetic words:

> But from this Grant I infer . . . that the Soveraigne [sic], original, and foundation of civill power lies in the people (whom they must needs meane by the civill power distinct from the Government set up). And if so, that a People may erect and establish what forme of Government seemes to them most meete for their civill condition: It is evident that such Governments as are by them erected and established, have no more power, nor for no longer time, then the civill power or people consenting and agreeing shall betrust them with. This is cleare not only in Reason, but in the experience of

all common-weales, where the people are not deprived of their naturall freedome by the power of Tyrants.[3]

Less than a century after Roger Williams died, and less than two decades after Edwards died, many Americans saw a developing threat to their liberty.

Self-Evident Truths

George III was a popular king in England. As monarchs go, he was probably more benevolent than most. But too much power in the hands of one man, even a well-intentioned man, can lead to arrogance and harsh, mercenary decisions. Such was the case with King George and his army, at least as viewed by a growing number of Americans. This perceived arrogance was leading Americans to contemplate revolt.

The Americans were irked by several British policies, including an edict prohibiting American settlements west of the Appalachians. But the biggest issue was taxes. (It seems that some things haven't changed much, even today.) Many Americans began to join together to make known their opposition, and to subvert the British edicts. This opposition caused the British to see what they perceived as a need to increase their military presence. Insult was added to injury when many of the colonists were forced to open their homes to house and feed the growing British army. This issue was so divisive that many of the churches began to address it. At this time, churches had become one of the major community, social, and political influences in colonial America.

At first, the colonists were divided as to what method should be pursued in opposing the British intrusions into their new lives as Americans. But on July 4, 1776, the Second Continental Congress published its Declaration of Independence from British rule, stating, "But when a long train of abuses and usurpations, pursuing invariably the same Object evinces a design to reduce them under absolute Despotism, it is their right, it is their duty, to throw off such government, and to provide new Guards for their future security." The revolution from British interference and control was at hand. This revolution would bring to the forefront, many examples of Americans who personified the best of American values. We can see this as we look at the lives of a few of our colonial heroes.

America's First Reluctant Hero

Despite Parson Mason Weems's popular legends, there is no credible record that the man who was about to become the leader of the newly formed American militia, ever chopped down a cherry tree, and then, compelled by honesty and remorse, confessed the deed to his father. But this character of honesty and courage was revealed in many other real-life incidents.

One such example started on a cold autumn night in 1753, when Virginia's Lieutenant Governor Robert Dinwidie sent his adjutant, twenty year-old George Washington, to Virginia's northern neck and eastern shore on a dangerous mission. The young adjutant was to lead a party of seven men to Fort Le Boeuf in Pennsylvania essentially to tell the French to get out of the Ohio Valley, or else face the wrath of the colonists. Undeterred, the French told Washington and his party they had no intention of leaving. In fact, they intended to take full possession of the Ohio River and exert a greater French military presence.

On the return trip from these encounters, Washington faced many perils to his life. There was the Indian's arrow that narrowly missed him. Then, as they crossed the Allegheny River in a makeshift raft, he fell into the icy river from which he pulled himself, got back into the raft and onto shore. Although he very nearly froze to death that night, he did not allow himself to be sidetracked but went on to complete his mission with complete personal commitment. In the ensuing French and Indian War, Washington's military skills and bravery continued to be developed and honed. Later, they became a strong, personal example that would provide courage to thousands of American militiamen who would leave their families and homes to wage a war for the American freedom and independence, we still enjoy today.

Twenty-two years later, with another war imminent, Washington selflessly recommended General Andrew Lewis, a fellow Virginian, to lead the colonial forces. But on June 15, 1775, against his recommendations, the Second Continental Congress unanimously chose Washington to lead the army. The men of the Congress chose him largely because they recognized his courage and stamina under pressure. Yet when appointed leader of the colonial forces, we see the level of his commitment. Washington refused to accept any payment for his military duties other than reimbursements for expenses.

Although there is some dispute about the earnestness and degree of Washington's religious beliefs and his participation in church services before the war, the images of him kneeling in prayer for guidance during the war are clearly part of the stories about the battles told by his men. Like most of his contemporaries, George Washington (regardless of his convictions about each) found his life influenced by the fundamentals of the Christian faith—for he was a product of his time. And, although that era was falling under the rationalistic influence of the Enlightenment, it was still heavily influenced by centuries of Christian traditions of honor and morality and, more recently, by the first Great Awakening a quarter-century before.

Although Washington is not generally considered to have been a great military strategist which led him to make plenty of mistakes, not the least of which was putting too much faith in his often timid subordinate officers, he had many qualities that often proved to be his greatest assets. But one that led to what was probably his greatest triumph may very well have come in response to his humble petitions to God. Here is one such example.

After several forceful British victories, British Admiral Howe withdrew to New York, confident in the soon demise of the American forces. On Christmas night, 1776, Washington, with a force of just twenty-four hundred men, totally surprised the Hessian mercenaries at Trenton, killing their commander and taking more than one thousand prisoners. As a result, British General Cornwallis and eight thousand soldiers, hurried to Trenton. After a brief skirmish with Washington's army, Cornwallis decided to wait until the next morning to "bag the old fox."

But during the night, the wind shifted and the wet roads froze (coincidence or providence?), allowing Washington and his army to quietly retreat. But "the old fox" (as General Washington became known by the enemy) slyly left the campfires burning, giving the appearance that nothing had changed. The Americans then sneaked around behind Cornwallis's troops and, in a surprise attack, gained a decisive victory over the larger British force. Washington's commitment to petition God may have been one of his greatest military strategies.

Following several subsequent, important British victories, Washington would have to face a different battle, however. These defeats led to internal intrigues among the American command, and some even favored a plan to wrest leadership of the American forces from Washington. But when Washington and his army, along with the help of five thousand French regulars, secured Cornwallis's surrender on October 19, 1781, his position as the clear leader of the American forces was solidified, and the American war for independence, practically speaking, was over.

However, the real story of any war is not in the lives and (relative) hardships of its leaders but in the very real hardships and endurance of the unheralded troops and civilians. The Continental Army endured terrible afflictions, not the least of which was lack of provisions. Next to death by enemy fire, it could be said that the American soldiers' worst enemy was death by starvation.

This enemy was described when Colonel Huntington included these words in a letter to his father, dated December 21, 1778:

> The people of Connecticut when at this Post, tell us, the Army must be made good, and the Country are all of that opinion, and yet do nothing. If you mean to do anything, do it soon. Convince us that you have not forgot us, which we have some reason to believe. Almost two years have passed, when we have been buoyed up with Promises at Loose Ends, (by the people in General). If you intend to feed us any Longer with Promises, you must at Least have some formality in passing them.

But the citizens at home could do little to help. They, too, were struggling with privation and hardships. But into this story of distress fits another amazing, but little-known, true story of provision.

Despite all of these hardships, these men, most of whom were untrained civilian soldiers, triumphantly and courageously faced all of the enemies at hand. They were willing to pay seemingly any price to secure freedom and independence from British tyranny for themselves, their families, and future generations of Americans.

During the very same long, cold winter that Colonel Huntington wrote his nearly desperate letter to his father, Washington's troops were huddling outside Philadelphia at Valley Forge. Many already had died from starvation and exposure to the elements, and many more were in danger of suffering the same fate. The war might have ended there with the fight for independence crushed. But the Oneida Indians walked hundreds of miles from their homes, bringing six hundred bushels of dried corn to the starving army. Among all the confederated but independent tribes of the Iroquois nation, only the Oneida and the Tuscarora sided with the colonists. The Oneida were an industrious people, and they were successful farmers. As an independent tribe, the Oneida appreciated the colonists' desire for self-determination. They fed and nursed the Americans back to health, and the fight continued. (Coincidence or providence?)

These Americans, from all walks of life and a wide variety of faiths, fed by a tribe of sympathetic Indians, epitomized the true principle of pluralism—respect for one another. They were different, yet they were drawn together by the common bond of a quest for freedom. How ironic that these Indians who assisted in the cause of freedom would soon be displaced from their lands and have their culture destroyed by those whom they helped to protect.

Reluctant Hero Becomes Reluctant President

In the months directly following the war, Washington lobbied the Continental Congress in Philadelphia, entreating the members to pay his army their back wages. During this battle, another insight is given into Washington's values. Before long, the great leader discovered that Colonel Lewis Nicola had written and circulated a letter with a plan for Washington to use the army to make himself king. Washington was outraged at such a suggestion, and he vividly made his anger known.

Two days before Christmas in 1783, Washington resigned his commission as leader of the fledgling country's young but victorious army. The next day he arrived back at Mt. Vernon, ready to resume his life as a gentleman-farmer. He did just that until May of 1787, when he was called to a gathering of all the states whose representatives were meeting in Philadelphia to "render the Constitution of the Federal Government adequate to the exigencies of the Union." He went reluctantly as one of Virginia's five delegates. Not surprisingly, the reluctant war hero and man of moral values was unanimously chosen to be president of the Constitutional Convention.

The country, like the Convention, needed a leader—a president. The reluctant hero was again the unanimous choice of the first electoral college. (What a contrast between Washington's character and the actions of our present-day presidents!) Read these words from Washington's first Inaugural Address, given April 30, 1789:

> Among the vicissitudes incident to life no event could have filled me with greater anxieties than that [his election as the United States' first president] of which the notification was transmitted by your order. . . . All I dare hope is that if, in executing this task, I have been too

much swayed by a grateful remembrance of former instances, or by an affectionate sensibility to this transcendent proof of the confidence of my fellow-citizens, and have thence too little consulted my incapacity as well as disinclination for the weighty and untried cares before me, my error will be palliated by the motives which mislead me, and its consequences be judged by my country with some share of the partiality in which they originated.

The reluctant hero was humbled by the trust of his fellow Americans and by the task set before him. Despite his reservations, Washington was true to his commitment and served this country well in caring for "the weighty and untried cares before" him.

In an era in which many politicians greedily vie for sound-bite coverage so they can voice platitudes about important issues, while feigning the appropriate emotion for the moment, only to run off and insult their constituents by their hypocritical behavior, how refreshing it would be to have a leader with our first president's honesty and humility and commitment to his constituents.

The Price of Freedom

Sometimes we may lose sight of some of the extreme examples of sacrifice made by some to secure our freedom. We have seen examples from the life of George Washington and from the lives of the brave and noble warriors who fought with him to secure our liberty. We even saw how a native Indian tribe participated in helping win the freedom we enjoy today. There are, however, many unsung heroes whose willing sacrifice became part of the cement that would bind our nation together. Some were among the signers of the Declaration of Independence.

Most of us have heard of a few of the more famous of the signers of the Declaration of Independence: Samuel Adams, John Adams, Thomas Jefferson, Benjamin Franklin, and, of course, John Hancock. But many of the fifty-six signers were less well known and have now become obscure to most Americans. But those men who signed the great document on July 2, 1776, (yes, only John Hancock, the president of the Congress, and Charles Thompson, the secretary of the Congress, signed it on the fourth) did so at great self-peril.

This declaration was considered by England to be an act of treason, and its signers would be considered traitors. The penalty for treason against the king was death by hanging. According to legend, however, John Hancock quipped, "Gentlemen, we must be unanimous; there must be no pulling in different ways; we must all hang together." To which Franklin was said to reply, "Yes, we must indeed hang together or most assuredly we will hang separately."

Indeed, the declaration they signed included the following words: "And for the support of this Declaration, with a firm Reliance on the Protection of divine Providence, we mutually pledge to each other our Lives, our Fortunes, and our sacred Honor."

As it turned out, nine of those who signed the Declaration of Independence died from wounds or illnesses suffered during the war for independence. Five more were captured or imprisoned during the war. Seventeen lost everything they owned and died penniless.

Others faced even more personal sacrifices. According to T. R. Ferenbach, in his book *Greatness to Spare: The Heroic Sacrifices of the Men who Signed the Declaration of Independence*, two of Abraham Clark's sons (Clark was from

New Jersey) were captured by the British and imprisoned in a floating hell hole.

Because their father was a signer, the Clarks were selected for especially brutal treatment. Thomas Clark, a captain of artillery, was put in solitary confinement and starved. He managed to stay alive only because other prisoners pushed bread to him through his key hole.

The British told Abraham Clark of his boys' fate and offered to release his boys if Clark deserted the patriots' cause. He refused. Further, he did not bring the matter to the attention of the Congress where he sat, and he asked for no special consideration from the military.

The examples of selfless sacrifice and commitment to moral principles were the hallmark character trait of those people who were the true foundation of this great country. Had the grand words of this country's founding documents not been forged in the life examples of these men and women, we would not be able to experience America the beautiful. Had it not been for their sacrifice and willingness to live by high moral standards, our America would not have attained its greatness. It is as though their lives provided the cement that would bind the strength needed for our founding governmental document. We should never forget that what made those law's work—and what still makes them work today—is the lives of those who are willing to add their commitment and sacrifice to making them work. America still needs such people today!

CHAPTER 2

THE BUILDING BLOCKS OF AMERICA

Employed in the service of my country abroad during the whole of these transactions, I first saw the Constitution in a foreign country. I read it with great satisfaction, as the result of good heads prompted by good hearts, as an experiment better adapted to the genius, character, situation, and relations of this nation and country than any which had ever been proposed or suggested

—*John Adams*
Inaugural speech

Securing the Blessings of Liberty

If President Washington was awed by the immensity of the task of leading a new nation, he could find solace in the strength and abilities of his fellow leaders. Together with fifty-four other delegates— including Jefferson, Madison, Hamilton, and Franklin—Washington had drafted and signed the Constitution of the United States of America two and a half years before his election. That document has guided this country for more than two centuries and has been largely responsible for America's relative security and stability. The Declaration of Independence, published eleven years earlier than the Constitution, had served to proclaim the new country's liberty. The newly approved Constitution would serve to maintain the liberties won by those who gave their lives gaining America's independence.

While the Constitutional Convention was under way in Philadelphia, a local citizen who identified himself only as "Harrington," wrote a letter to Philadelphia newspapers about the drafting of the Constitution and those who were composing it. The following is an excerpt from that letter:

> Perhaps no age or country ever saw more wisdom, patriotism, and probity united in a single assembly than we now behold in a Convention of the States. . . . Under the present weak, imperfect and distracted government of Congress—anarchy, poverty, infamy and slavery await the United States. Under such a government as will probably be formed by the present Convention, Americans may yet enjoy peace, safety, liberty and glory.

Harrington was right; Americans would yet enjoy the blessings provided by the wisdom of the framers of the Constitution. But the establishment of that great document would not prove to be a simple task.

During those formative years, the country's leaders were divided between Federalists (those who called for a limited central government) and non-Federalists (those who were so wary of autocratic control that they wanted no central government). During the years following the war for independence from England, the strong confederation of states that had been united by the common cause of independence, began to unravel. States often ignored the pre-Constitutional Confederation Congress's resolutions and refused to pay their share of expenses. Thomas Jefferson wrote, "I find . . . pride of independence [of states from one another] taking a deep and dangerous hold on the hearts of individual states."

John Jay, Secretary of Foreign Affairs and a wealthy member of Congress, wrote the following to George Washington:

> What I most fear is that the better kind of people (by which I mean the people who are orderly and industrious, who are content with their situations, and not uneasy in their circumstances) will be led, by the insecurity of property, the loss of confidence in their rulers, and the want of public faith and rectitude, to consider the charms of liberty as imaginary and delusive.

(The dangers expressed in this statement are ones that Americans today still need to be on guard against.)

Washington's reply was firm in his support of America's unique republican government.

> What astonishing changes a few years are capable of producing! I am told that even respectable characters speak of a monarchical form of government without horror. From thinking proceeds speaking, and thence to acting is often but a single step. But how irrevocable and tremendous! What a triumph for our enemies to verify their predictions! What a triumph for the advocates of despotism to find out that we are incapable of governing ourselves, and that systems founded on the basis of equal liberty are merely ideal and fallacious!

Luther Martin, a Constitutional Convention delegate, at one point stated, "I'll be hanged if the people of Maryland ever agree to [the Constitution]."

But to Martin's statement, Daniel of St. Thomas Jenifer, another Maryland delegate, replied, "I advise you to stay in Philadelphia lest you should be hanged."

It was going to take a very special, indeed, a peerless dedication to establish the defining document that would provide this new country with the unity it would need for strength and justice, while at the same time preserving local independence, so as to preclude the type of tyranny possible at the federal level.

After long arguments and deliberations, Delaware became the first state to ratify the Constitution on December 7, 1787. Slowly, gradually, the other states followed, until on November 19, 1789, North Carolina became the twelfth to ratify it. At that point, Rhode Island was the last holdout. Six months later, the US Senate passed a bill that broke off commercial relations with the tiny northern state. On May 29, 1790, by a narrow margin, Rhode Island became the last state to ratify the US Constitution.

The original US Constitution is not a long document; it has just seven articles. The first article establishes the House of Representatives and the Senate, defining their duties and their limitations. The second article establishes the office of the presidency, again defining the duties and limitations. The third article does for the judicial branch of the federal government what the first and second articles do for the legislative and executive branches. The fourth article deals with the rights of the individual states within the union.

With the wisdom to recognize their fallibility in a changing world, the framers of the Constitution allowed for amendments to the document they were developing in the fifth article. This article established the methods for amendments. The very next article declares this same Constitution to be the "supreme law of the land." All members of all branches of the previously established government will be bound by an oath to support the Constitution. America would be a nation of laws, not of men. The seventh, and final, article established the requirement for ratifying the document: approval by delegates of nine of the thirteen states. (Two years later, in 1789, the first ten amendments, known as the Bill of Rights, were added.)[4]

It was a simple document, but it has proven to be profound in its abilities to guide this country through several crises and to maintain the freedoms of Americans from all walks of life and all cultural backgrounds.

Here is a sampling of quotations about the Constitution from some of America's first leaders:

If it be asked, What is the most sacred duty and the greatest source of our security in a Republic? The answer would be, An inviolable respect for the Constitution and laws -the first growing out of the last. It is by this, in a great degree, that the rich and powerful are to be restrained from enterprises against the common liberty. . . .

A sacred respect for the constitutional law is the vital principle, the sustaining energy of a free government.

—*Alexander Hamilton*

The conception of [the Constitution] and the deliberate union of so great and various a people in such a plan is, without partiality or prejudice, if not the greatest exertion of human understanding, the greatest single effort of national deliberation that the world has ever seen.

—*John Adams*

This government, the offspring of our own choice uninfluenced and unawed, adopted upon full investigation and mature deliberation, completely free in its principles, in the distribution of its powers, uniting security with energy, and containing within itself a provision for its own amendment, has a just claim to your confidence and your support. Respect for its authority, compliance with its Laws, acquiescence in its measures, are duties enjoined by the fundamental maxims of true liberty.

—*George Washington*

Over the years and decades, the founding document on which our country's government was built, the Constitution of these United States, would withstand many bumps, barbs, and arrows that would come her way. But the heavy-howitzer assault would not arrive until nearly two hundred years after its publication (as we will see more clearly in section 2 of this book, "Researching Our Decline").

We need to keep in focus, however, that it will be new examples of heroism and selfless commitment that will provide the bulwark to enable this grand form of government to weather the modern storms and to continue grandly and gloriously into the twenty-first century, as it did in its first two centuries. Who will rise to the occasion and be the heroes of the twenty-first century?

Patriots of a Higher Calling

While American patriots were fighting for their liberty in this land, others, many of whom nonetheless lent their support to the cause, questioned the apparent contradiction of fighting against a seeming economic slavery to England, while holding thousands of others to a literal slavery because of their skin color. Samuel Hopkins, one of Johnathan Edwards's closest friends, who later served as pastor of a Congregational church in Newport, Rhode Island, wrote in a pamphlet he sent to members of the Continental Congress:

> [Negroes] see the slavery the Americans dread as worse than death, is lighter than a feather, compared to their

heavy doom; and [this so-called enslavement by Parliament] can be called liberty and happiness, when contrasted with the most abject slavery and unutterable wretchedness to which they are subjected.[5]

And others, such as Isaac Backus, argued that there was a contradiction involved in fighting for freedom from England, while smaller, less established American Christian groups like his own Baptists were mistreated by the larger, more established Congregationalists.

America had won its freedom from England; now it needed to gain freedom from itself.

The Second Great Awakening

Despite the first Great Awakening a couple of decades prior to the Revolution, by the time the war began, the colonists' church membership, by some historians' reckoning, was less than 30 percent. (Some have estimated that at that time in New England, the figure may have been more like 5 percent.) As a result, the morals of the post-Revolution society were in a state of despair, and various social problems became rampant.

Of the time directly following the war, historian Edwin Orr wrote:

> The Methodists were losing more members than they were gaining. The Baptists said that they had their most wintry season. The Presbyterians in general assembly deplored the nation's ungodliness. . . . The Lutherans were so languishing that they discussed uniting with the Episcopalians who were even worse off.[6]

If the failure of many to respond in repentance to the message of the gospel had deprived them of the good life

41

in their future eternity, their very real response to the Christian message of selfless devotion had struck a chord that would resound to the benefit of their progeny. Americans today still enjoy the fruits of these earlier Americans' self-sacrifice.

But dedicated ministers were not content to watch and bless the work of building a great nation while the moral fiber of the new American society declined. Nor were many of those same ministers willing to look the other way while entire races were exploited to help build a great nation—a nation that would share few of the benefits that greatness would afford with those exploited peoples. The second Great Awakening was about to begin.

This was the era of Francis Asbury, the pioneer circuit rider; James McGready, originator of camp meetings; Lyman Beecher, founder of the American Bible Society and father of Harriet Beecher Stowe, who wrote *Uncle Tom's Cabin*; and of Charles Finney, the great evangelist and abolitionist. It was the era of the development of the concomitant concerns for the now and the hereafter.

If Johnathan Edwards personified the first Great Awakening, Charles Finney, with his two-pronged ministry of converting souls and converting society, embodied the second. Author Leon McBeth wrote, "Perhaps the greatest leader of the second Great Awakening was Charles G. Finney, the converted lawyer credited with transforming the style of evangelism in America."

The second Great Awakening is generally acknowledged to have begun in Maine in 1790. This second wave of American revitalization was more prolonged and more encompassing than the first. Finney's conversion to his Christian faith took place some thirty years after the event began.

(Some might almost conclude that there was a distinct third Great Awakening, because the second one went through a "cooling" during and after the War of 1812. But a renewal of change began to sweep across the people of this newly formed nation, so as to once again bring change, vigor, and purpose in the decades of the 1820s and 1830s.)

Of his conversion, Finney wrote: "I was converted on the morning of the tenth of October, 1821. In the evening of the same day, I received overwhelming baptisms (infillings) of the Holy Ghost, that went through me, as it seemed to me, body and soul. I immediately found myself endued with such power from on high that a few words dropped here and there to individuals were the means of their immediate conversion."[7]

Perhaps more than any American before—or since— Charles Finney saw the need to minister to whole people, body and soul. He once said, "Many professed Christians hold that nothing is needful but simply faith and repentance, and thus faith may exist without real benevolence and good works. The grand requisition which God makes upon man is that he become truly benevolent."

As the seven earlier described values came to life during the first Great Awakening, along with the spirit of self-sacrifice and fortitude forged during the Revolution, the spirit of personal change and social justice was birthed in the second Great Awakening.

The leaders of this second Great Awakening were responsible for a myriad of social works, such as the abolition movement, as well as establishing many of America's colleges and universities. But more subtle, and just as profound, was the impact of the second Great Awakening on the general social fabric and structure of the country. Donald

Scott, a professor at Queens College and at City University of New York, wrote the following in a paper about the second Great Awakening, titled "Evangelicalism as a Social Movement."

> Conversion thus not only brought communicants into a new relationship to God; it also brought them into a new and powerful institutional fabric that provided them with personal discipline, a sense of fellowship, and channeled their benevolent obligations in appropriate directions. Aggressively exploiting a wide variety of new print media, evangelicals launched their own newspapers and periodicals and distributed millions of devotional and reform tracts.

This social awakening gave impetus and cohesion to apply the practical aspects of the reform movement, which helped to distribute the benefits of America's greatness that sprang from those seven basic principles I outlined in chapter 1. These basic moral principles have formed the spiritual and moral infrastructure of this great country.

The very foundations of our nation are based on the moral character and hard work of individuals and communities. Consequently, governmental programs have never, nor can they ever, produce the kind of truly profound and beneficial changes that have swept across America during the two Great Awakenings. America will remain strong as everyday Americans continue to give themselves in true sacrifice to foster the moral foundations and to help build in it the lives of successive generations. When the God-created greatness of each individual American is esteemed, encouraged, and held high, then and only then, does the concept of a government of the people, by the people, and for the people have any significance.

Oh, that America today would once again experience the fire of change and revival that twice swept across this land to produce a great and enduring nation and would see a new rebirth of a great nation that will endure the pressures and challenges of a new millennium—the twenty-first century!

CHAPTER 3

THE PIONEER SPIRIT AND VISION THAT FORGED AMERICA

Searcher of hearts,
It is a good day to me when thou givest me
a glimpse of myself.
Sin is my greatest evil,
but thou art my greatest good.
I have cause to loathe myself,
and not to seek self-honour,
for no one desires to commend his own dunghill.
My country, family, church
fare worse because of my sins,
for sinners bring judgment in thinking sins are small,
or that God is not angry with them.
Let me not take other good men as my example
and think that I am good because I am like them.
For all good men are not so good as thou desirest,
are not always consistent,
do not always follow holiness,
do not feel eternal good in sore affliction.
Show me how to know when a thing is evil
which I think is right and good,

how to know when what is lawful
comes from an evil principle,
such as desire for reputation or wealth by usury.
Give me grace to recall my needs,
my lack of knowing thy will in Scripture,
of wisdom to guide others,
of daily repentance, want of which keeps thee at bay,
of the spirit of prayer, having words without love,
of zeal for thy glory, seeking my own ends,
of joy in thee and thy will,
of love to others.
And let me not lay my pipe too short of the fountain,
never touching the eternal spring,
never drawing down water from above.
—VALLEY OF VISION
A book of Puritan prayers and devotions

A Pipe Sometimes Short of the Fountain

I would be dishonest to state, or imply, that the founding of our great nation was always, and in all ways, based on Americans' godly responses to biblical mandates. Our forefathers made their share of mistakes and sins. As we already saw, many of the early settlers were not Christians. And many who really were Christians, like us, still sinned—sometimes out of ignorance, sometimes because of self-will. Then, as always, sin extracted a heavy price on the sinners and those sinned against. As always, their sins rippled, going out as waves from their source and beyond them.

By the time of his arrival in the colonies from England, Roger Williams, once a Puritan himself, was a Christian nonconformist. One of his primary disagreements with the Plymouth Puritans had to do with ownership of land. Unlike most of the Puritans, Williams believed that to gain Indian land, settlers must legally purchase it from the Indians.

How could the Puritans justify taking land from the Indians by force? Without getting too deeply into the Puritan theological philosophy, which differed greatly from Williams's own philosophy, it seems to me that the crux of the problem that led the Puritans to take the Indian land without consideration or payment, sprung from their confused view about two kingdoms—a worldly kingdom and a heavenly one. Sometimes, when the greed of the moment would seem to dictate, they might evoke the worldly philosophy of their new colonial kingdom, and then justify it by teaching that they needed the land to further the ends of a heavenly kingdom.

They saw their community as "the city on the hill," God's divinely established kingdom rule on earth. Consequently, that which interfered with the establishment of that kingdom needed to be removed. Although greed may also have played a part in the motivation of some Puritans, most were probably real believers whose "pipes" may have unfortunately strayed [a bit too far] from the fountain of eternal water.

Roger Williams, on the other hand, and those who followed in his tradition, called for a clear separation between the world-oriented kingdom and a truly spiritual kingdom, which exists, and of necessity, functions within the world's kingdom. Williams saw Christians' attempts to enforce God's kingdom rule on those who would acquiesce, and to physically oppose those who would resist, as counterproductive to the spread of the gospel and as offensive to God. Williams wrote the following in 1644 as part of a plea for religious liberty:

> It is the will and command of God that (since the coming of his Son the Lord Jesus) a permission of the most

paganish, Jewish, Turkish, or antichristian consciences and worships, be granted to all men in all nations and countries; and they are only to be fought against with that sword which is only (in soul matters) able to conquer, to wit, the sword of God's Spirit, the Word of God.

And if the Puritans' dealings with the Native Americans were less than honorable, due to a mistaken theology and personal greed, the plantation owners' and merchants' treatment of Africans brought here as slaves also was an atrocity. Sadly, many of those who justified this awful sin, misused the Bible to try and defend their actions. Again, some (perhaps more so than among the Puritans) were motivated strictly by greed, but some were real Bible-believers who were operating with "pipes" too short to receive adequate sustenance from the spring of eternal water.

And, although nothing short of God's grace can atone for the sin of one race of people enslaving another, the trials faced by those enslaved Africans served to increase the character and true faith upon which our nation was founded. This time of trial and tribulation developed some of this nations' greatest—if often overlooked—heroes.

In 1845, George Moses Horton recounted some of his life as a slave in North Carolina during the first half of the nineteenth century. Even as a young boy, Horton had a fondness for words, he taught himself to read and write! And, in spite of the less-than-Christian surroundings provided on his master's farm, Horton sought the moral high road. He wrote the following of his master's influence on his fellow slaves:

Those days resembled the days of martyrdom, and all christendom seemed to be relapsing into dissipation; and libertinism, obscenity and profanation were in their full career; and the common conversation was impregnated with droll blasphemy. In those days sensual gratification was prohibited by few; for drinking, I had almost said, was a catholic [universal] toleration, and from 1800 to 1810 there was scarcely a page of exemplary conduct laid before my eyes.

And that same self-taught slave, George Moses Horton, penned this inspired poem (among many others).

Sing, O ye ransom'd, shout and tell
What God has done for ye;
The horses and their riders fell
And perish'd in the sea.

Look back, the vain Egyptian dies
Whilst plunging from the shore;
He groans, he sinks, but not to rise,
King Pharaoh is no more.

These observations of those who lived during these times of slavery almost give us a picture of moral decay (profuse obscenities, excessive drunkenness, and rampant sexual lust) looking to find gratification at the expense of others weaker than they (either in society or physically). It is almost as if when we disregard respect for all men and women of all races, colors, and creeds, we lose part of the moral fiber that keeps us personally free from personal addictions and excesses.

Thomas H. Jones was a slave for forty-three years, and of him, the great abolitionist William Lloyd Garrison wrote, "[He was] exemplary in life—a servant and minister of Jesus Christ. . . ."

Jones wrote the following anecdote in an account of his life as a slave:

With great eagerness, I snatched every moment I could get, morning, noon and night, for study. I began to read; and, oh, how I loved to study, and to dwell on the thoughts which I gained from reading. About this time, I read a piece in my book about God. It said that "God, who sees and knows all our thoughts, loves the good and makes them happy; while he is angry with the bad, and will punish them for all their sins." This made me feel very unhappy, because I was sure I was not good in the sight of God. I thought about this, and couldn't get it out of my mind a single hour. So I went to James Galley, a colored man, who exhorted the slaves sometimes on Sunday, and told him my trouble, asking, "what shall I do?" He told me about Jesus, and told me I must pray the Lord to forgive me and help me to be good and happy. So I went home, and went down cellar and prayed, but I found no relief, no comfort for my unhappy mind. I felt so bad that I could not study my book. My master saw that I looked very unhappy, and he asked me what ailed me. I did not dare now to tell a lie, for I wanted to be good, that I might be happy. So I told my master just how it was with me; and then he swore terribly at me, and said he would whip me if I did not give over praying. He said there was no heaven and no hell, and that Christians are all hypocrites. . . .

But despite this, and a near lifetime of hardships unimaginable to present-day Americans, Thomas Jones learned to trust God and many of God's servants who helped him. Near the end of the narrative in which he told of his trials as a slave, he wrote these words: "Tribulation and distress, with many kind dealings of Providence and wonderful deliverances, have since been my lot. I hope to be able to tell in another narrative, of my adventures after the close of this story, of the kindness of friends and the goodness of God."

Chief among those friends of Thomas Jones, and of all slaves, was the American Anti-Slavery Society. The society sought to end slavery throughout America, but at the same time, to preserve states' rights. Article 2 of the Anti-Slavery Society's Constitution included the following:

> The objects of this Society are the entire abolition of slavery in the United States. While it admits that each state, in which slavery exists, has, by the Constitution of the United States, the exclusive right to legislate in regard to abolition in said state, it shall aim to convince all our fellow-citizens, by arguments addressed to their understandings and consciences, that Slaveholding is a heinous crime in the sight of God. . . .

In the Sight (and Name) of God

Those Pilgrims who first arrived at Plymouth aboard the Mayflower probably never had any intention of enslaving another people. They knew all too well the dread of domination by others. They began their Mayflower Compact with the words, "In the name of God . . ." They went on to state that their enterprise was "undertaken for the Glory of God, and advancement of the Christian Faith. . . ."

The Articles of Confederation of the United Colonies of New England (1631–1681) began, "Whereas we all came into these parts of America with one and the same end and aim, namely, to advance the Kingdom of our Lord Jesus Christ and to enjoy the liberties of the gospel in purity with peace. . . ."

In spite of the personal sins of some early Americans and the corporate sins of early America, many of our forebears were people of great faith and moral character. This was a country infused with, and permeated by, Christian morality—even among those who were not true believers. Many of our founding fathers—those who wrote and signed the documents that declared and protect our freedoms— were Deists who rejected many basic Christian doctrines relating to Christ. However, they were also a people conscious of God's ultimate judgment, and they had a keen sense of what was morally right and wrong.

I believe they were more willing than most Americans today to make hard personal sacrifices for the sake of their neighbors, their country, and future generations of Americans. I remember the emotions I felt at seeing the actual Plymouth Rock a number of years ago. Looking around at the restored examples of the self-sacrifice of these great early Americans was so overwhelming when I compared it to the America of today, where we demand immediate gratification without any need for personal discipline or sacrifice.

A Hard Road to Another Promised Land

At the close of the Revolutionary War with England, America's non-Indian population (including about 600,000 slaves) was just under four million, and very few of them lived anywhere west of the Appalachians. Daniel Boone, perhaps America's most legendary adventurer, was among the first to investigate the great beyond to the west. Born in 1734, Boone, while still a child, was befriended by Indians. That began his life as an outdoorsman and explorer.

When he was thirty-three years old, Boone spent a winter at Salt Spring, Kentucky. A year and a half later, he joined his friend John Finley and four other men, and set out on what became a two-year exploration that took them as far as present-day Louisville. The men spent the winter of 1769–70, living in a cave. This trip, and many that followed, despite many hardships, played a large part in the development of the United States. And it showed the moral fiber of this great mountain man.

Boone became an agent of a Carolina trading company, and in 1775, he was commissioned to establish a road for colonists to travel to Kentucky. At the end of the road, he built a fort and stockade that became known as Boonesboro. Boone and the residents of Boonesboro suffered many attacks during the Revolutionary War. They also weathered many hardships and attacks from unfriendly Indians, to build and protect this oasis in the frontier colonial desert. This oasis eventually became a permanent settlement and a stopover on the westward migration, furthering the building of our great nation. As was true in so many events surrounding the founding of our great nation, it was by the will and commitments of its founders, as well as providential help in facing war and deprivation, that enabled this settlement to become a stepping stone to the building of a great nation.

If Daniel Boone was the quintessential adventurer, Meriwether Lewis and William Clark were the fundamental American explorers. When they finally returned home to a hero's welcome in 1806, they were just thirty-one and thirty-five years old respectively. They had been gone two and one-third years and had been given up for dead. With the dangers they faced, it was perhaps, just short of a miracle that they, and their entire party, didn't perish during the adventure.

In 1803, the country was not long out of its infancy. But President Thomas Jefferson saw that the country's future was in the West. Just before sending the explorers, who named their group the Corps of Discovery, the president made one of the world's all-time great land deals; he bought 828,000 square miles of earth, trees, water, and other resources from

France. In what became known as the Louisiana Purchase, Napoleon sold the massive parcel to the young nation for less than three cents per acre. The Corps of Discovery would work its way west through the newly purchased land and beyond, all the way to the Pacific Ocean.

The Corps of Discovery struggled westward, often through harsh weather and illnesses. They encountered huge, aggressive grizzly bears that seemed all but impervious to the lead balls fired by their long rifles. They enjoyed the hospitality of some friendly native tribes, and narrowly escaped the wrath of other tribes, such as the Lakotas, who tried to extort unreasonable tolls for passage through their lands. They overcame the nuisance of mosquito swarms and persevered over the imposing Rocky Mountains. After eighteen months of forcing themselves on, they were rewarded by their goal—the Pacific Ocean. Then came the long, wet winter.

Having arrived at their destination on November 7, the party knew it was the wrong time of year to turn around and start back. They built the Fort Clatsop stockade just south of the mouth of the Columbia River, near the site of present-day Astoria, Oregon. Two words best describe Oregon's north coast in the winter: *gray* and *wet*. That area doesn't get a lot of torrential downpours, but the drizzle and light rain is almost constant. And from November to June, sightings of the sun are more rare than sightings of Sasquatch.

So for more than five months, the Corps of Discovery lived on a diet that consisted of little more than elk meat and water and watched as their clothes and many of their belongings began to mildew and rot in the constant moisture. All they could do was wait.

They began their return trip on March 23, 1806, and arrived back in St. Louis exactly six months later. The Corps of Discovery had traveled six thousand miles of wilderness and had seen and recorded sights no white men had ever seen before. They were heroes. America had reached another milestone. The great westward expansion was beginning.

Not unlike their forebears who arrived in America two hundred years before, the pioneers traveled west for several reasons. Some, such as Marcus and Narcissa Whitman, followed their call from God to ministries in new lands. Many others were in search of riches or adventure. However, most were people of limited resources who held reluctant hope for a better future in a new land and a constant, if sometimes uneducated, simple faith in God to provide.

In 1840, thirty-four years after the Corps of Discovery returned to St. Louis, there were still just three states west of the Mississippi River. But in 1841, the first major group emigrated from the banks of the Missouri River on what was soon to become known as the Oregon Trail. By the time the exodus was complete some forty years later, nearly 400,000 people—many in wagons, but most on foot—would wear an indelible 2,170-mile road (the Oregon Trail) across the plains, over the mountains, and into the Oregon Territory.

Of the long, arduous walk, historian Merrill Mattes wrote, "Able-bodied children of all ages walked, and some walked clear across the United States; and frequently without shoes." Although the travelers faced any number of accidents and weather-related problems, according to Mattes, "the greatest single problem" was cholera. "And there was nothing they could do about it—if they got it they were dead." According to Mattes, "The trip for most people was an ordeal. More than they bargained for, I'm sure. But most of them had the guts to stick it out and get there or die in the effort."

Most of us today, in the age of microwaves, multilane highways, and McDonald's, are utterly without reference point for comprehending the hardships endured as a part of everyday life by our ancestors. Whether they were poor white settlers, slaves of African descent, or Native Americans, enduring harsh weather and watching their way of life erode around them, the discipline and perseverance of those who went before us through hardships and trials gave them a dignity and strength of character that is all too rare today.

Banana Blessings

Thanks to my grandmother, Nancy Guinn, I have witnessed that strength of character in a very personal way. (And thanks to her, I'll always have a special place in my heart—and in my diet—for bananas.) Grandma (who by the time of her death had forty-seven grandchildren, 111 great-grandchildren, and thirty-five great-great-grandchildren) always managed to find some "special time" just for me when our family would go to visit her in eastern Tennessee on our annual family vacations. Grandma and her family lived in what, by today's standards, would be considered a shabby old shack. They had little money and had to be frugal.

During my visits to Grandma, she and I would take our special walk through her carefully tended garden, and as we walked, she would stop and look around to make sure that we were alone. Then she would reach into her oversized apron pockets and almost magically bring forth two golden, ripe bananas. Those bananas became a symbol for me—a symbol that someone cared very much for me, and despite Grandma's lack of material things, she went out of her way to get that special fruit and to spend time alone with me.

I later learned how difficult Grandma's life had been. She had raised not just her own ten children, but also others from Grandpa's previous marriage. Yet she continued to cook and clean and tend and weed her garden every day until she was hospitalized shortly before her death at the age of ninety-three. Grandma once told me that taking care of her family was her job. It was a job she fulfilled with the greatest faithfulness, diligence, and most of all, love.

Grandma fought so many struggles to hang on to just one more day of life, so she could do her job here on earth. These included financial, health, and personal struggles. I am often saddened when I think of people today who want to give up or end their lives prematurely. I wonder how it might change their lives to have my grandma's pioneer spirit, purpose, and determination for life. I wonder what difference it would make if people today, like my grandma, had their jobs in life clearly defined and were willing to spend every day making sure they do those jobs to the best of their abilities.

I can't help but believe that with more modern-day Grandma Guinns as role models, there would also be more new-generation Americans willing to carry on her example of clarity of purpose for life and her insatiable desire to live a real life to its fullest benefit for all.

CHAPTER 4

PROTECTION
OF AMERICAN VALUES

Sixteen soldiers were exposed to fierce enemy machine-gun fire as they climbed the hill, but they made their way to the top with no casualties. Now they would attempt to descend the hill, unnoticed by the battery of enemy forces below them. Before the soldiers reached their objective, they arrived at a stream where they spotted twenty to thirty of the Kaiser's soldiers. The Germans had not seen the Americans. With the element of surprise, and a few well-aimed shots, the sixteen American soldiers gained the surrender of the surprised Germans. It was October 8, 1918—near the end of World War I.

But those shots alerted the German machine gunners, and they spotted the Americans. The machine gunners were no more than thirty yards away and they opened fire. Captors and prisoners hit the dirt, but six of the sixteen Americans had been killed, and three more, including the sergeant who was leading them, were badly injured. Of the remaining American soldiers, all but one were needed to guard the nearly thirty captives. That remaining soldier was the surest shot in all Tennessee—perhaps in all the world. He was Corporal Alvin C. York, and by the time he was done shooting, he had killed a couple dozen "Boches," as the Americans called the German soldiers.

York seemed invincible. His shooting was so deadly accurate that the awe-struck major of the group of German captives, who spoke English and who was accompanied by one of the American soldiers, put his hand on York's shoulder and said, "Don't shoot any more, and I'll make them surrender." And that's exactly what happened.

Corporal York and the remaining American soldiers marched their captives back toward the American lines. Incredibly, when other German soldiers in machine-gun nests saw their captive comrades, they decided resistance was futile, and they, too, surrendered to the small group of American soldiers led by Corporal York. By the time the contingent made its way back to the American lines, they were marching 132 German prisoners of war in front of them.

The story may sound too fantastic to be believed, but the events were independently investigated and verified. York, who was promoted to sergeant, returned to the States as a hero. This quiet, Tennessee mountain boy, who because of his religious convictions, had been a conscientious objector at the start of the war, was presented with America's highest military honor, the Congressional Medal of Honor.

But how many of today's Americans have ever heard of Sergeant York? Perhaps this poem partially explains why most Americans today have never heard of this great American.

> God and the soldier
> All men adore
> In time of trouble,
> And no more;
> For when war is over
> And things are righted,

God is neglected,
The old soldier slighted.

The anonymous poem above, found on an old sentry box on the island of Gibraltar, tells eloquently, and all too honestly, the way we tend to regard the heroes who put their lives on the line for their loved ones, their country, and the ideals that define their country. Those of us who have never fought in a war, who have never spent day after day for months or years shooting at nameless enemies (who were equally intent on killing us), probably can never understand the deep feelings and agonies of these soldiers—not even by watching the blockbuster movie *Saving Private Ryan*.

I have a friend whose father tells the story of a lecture he heard from his commanding officer before he and his fellow American soldiers of the Second Armored Division hit the Normandy beaches three days after D-day in World War II. The officer told the men, "If you survive this, the US government will take care of your medical needs for the rest of your life." *If you survive* . . . certainly not reassuring words to young men about to head off onto blood-spattered beaches and then into forests full of flying bullets and exploding artillery. But they were defending their country and saving the world from fascist tyranny.

Many of them did not survive. Many of those who did would need to rely on that promise of government care for their medical needs. Many returned with horrific injuries, including limbs lost to bullets, shrapnel, or frostbite. And that was just one story of one division in one war. Over the years, since America achieved its independence, more than two million of this country's bravest have given their lives defending America and its principles. Millions more have been lost or wounded.

There are those among us who believe no cause is worth going to war over. Some hold that belief because of their religious convictions. I respect them for that. And although I disagree with them, I would defend their rights to object to war, based on their principles and convictions. However, over the past few decades, a new breed of war protester has emerged. These people don't base their pacifism on deep religious or moral convictions, but simply on the notion that *nothing is worth fighting for*.

This view would permit a cruel despot to send armies to commit brutal genocide on a defenseless people, while we, despite our power to stop such brutality, turn the other way. This view would allow a tyrant or a terrorist to rob us of our freedom, because any type of life is better than death. I believe that the United States of America has fought too hard and sacrificed too much to ever give up the principles of liberty and righteousness that have become our hallmark. Let's take a look at some of the sacrifices past Americans—and our contemporaries—have made for the sake of our freedom and our values.

O'er the Land of the Free and the Home of the Brave

As with any war, there is no shortage of theories about the cause(s) of the War of 1812. Some see it as having been a simple case of America protecting its commerce rights. Others find more complicated reasons, some of which cast the United States in a less virtuous light. Without getting too deeply into the different views, I will say simply that the primary cause was the British sea blockade during Britain's struggle with Napoleon's France. American merchant ships were caught in the middle and were unable to carry on much of their trade. The stakes were raised when British ship captains began to seize American citizens (some of whom may have been British deserters) to man their ships.

Then on November 7, 1811, as an American force of eight hundred men, led by William Henry Harrison, was encamped near the Shawnee Indian village of Tippecanoe, a Shawnee shot one of Harrison's sentinels. (The Shawnee had formed something of an alliance with the British.) Harrison and his soldiers responded by attacking and destroying Tippecanoe. Tempers were heating up. The pot boiled, and on June 18, 1812, it erupted into a declaration of war by President James Madison.

Although the War of 1812 would not be remembered in the same context as the war for independence, the Civil War, and the world wars, it should be remembered by all Americans for giving us our national anthem.

It took place during the Battle of Baltimore, September 11–15, 1814. British forces had burned Washington, DC, a month before. At six-thirty A.M. on September 13, British warships began bombarding Fort McHenry, near Baltimore. Americans in the fort, manned the cannons and returned fire. The British ships moved back out of the range of the fort's guns. But back on land, British Colonel Brooke planned a flanking movement on the American forces protecting Baltimore. Brooke needed a diversion. He called on the Royal Navy. But in order for the navy to distract the Americans, they had to move back within range of the fort's guns. When they did, the Americans scored several hits.

For twenty-five hours, cannon balls flew furiously back and forth between the ships and the fort. The story is told that the British were aiming at the American flag that stood high above Fort McHenry. As the British demolished the base holding the flag, the still–remaining soldiers would quickly jump in and manually hold up the flag, so that it would remain standing. The story goes on to describe that, through the night and into the next morning, countless numbers of soldiers would die, as one after another, they willingly gave up their lives to assure that their flag remained high. So many of them gave their lives on that spot to hold high the flag, that the mound of bodies finally kept the flag high and visible above the fort. Perhaps the details of this story are true. We do not fully know. What we do know is that brave and courageous men made whatever sacrifices were necessary to assure that our nation's flag stood proud and continued to wave throughout the battle.

We know this, because at seven the next morning, the Royal Navy withdrew and sailed downriver. Fort McHenry had withstood the assault, and soldiers in Fort McHenry had continued to keep the stars and stripes raised as the British left. Francis Scott Key was so inspired by these brave men and the still-waving flag, that he wrote the "Star-Spangled Banner," which would come to represent American courage through the years as our national anthem. Let us not forget the awesome price behind the words of this song when we next hear it sung.

Preservation of the Union

Thanks to Ken Burns' popular and masterfully produced series about the Civil War, titled very simply *The Civil War,* many Americans may know more about this part of America's history than of any other era. It's right that we should know about these four years that were truly a defining point for our country. As we saw in the previous chapter of this book, young America, for all its virtues and wisdom, made its share of mistakes. Not the least of those mistakes was the allowance of slavery. But at the outset of the Civil War, slavery was not the preeminent issue that divided our nation—at least not for those who were in power.

As the presidential election of 1860 neared, the Democratic Party split with those in the southern wing, nominating John C. Breckenridge of Kentucky, and those in the northern wing, nominating Stephen Douglas. Meanwhile, the recently formed Constitutional Union Party nominated John Bell, another southerner. The split of the Democrats, as well as the votes drawn from the South by Bell, allowed the Republicans to elect Abraham Lincoln as president. Lincoln and the Republicans had run on a platform that opposed further expansion of slavery (not abolition) and endorsed a Homestead Act, a protective tariff, and federal subsidies for internal improvements.

By the time of Lincoln's inauguration in March of 1861, seven southern states had seceded and begun the Confederate States of America, with Jefferson Davis as president.

Lincoln argued that those southern states were violating the law by seceding. On April 12, 1861, while federal soldiers were attempting to resupply Fort Sumter in Charleston, South Carolina, soldiers of the Confederate States fired artillery at the federal troops. On April 15, Lincoln called for additional troops to respond and quell the rebellion. Four more southern states responded by joining the Confederacy.

On paper, the war should have been no contest. The population in the North was more than twice that of the South. Moreover, nearly half of the South's population was made up of slaves who had no reason to hold any loyalties to the Confederacy. And the North had better manufacturing facilities.

But the South had such superior leaders for its army, that a war, which both sides thought would end quickly, wore on for four years. Most of us have at least heard of the famous and bloody battles: Chancellorsville, Vicksburg, Chickamuga, Chattanooga, The Wilderness Campaign, and of course, Gettysburg. By the end of the war on April 9, 1865, it is estimated that 620,000 Americans had given their lives.

There's no shortage of poignant stories from the Civil War. Many can be drawn directly from personal accounts and letters from soldiers. One of the most moving is the following letter, written by Major Sullivan Ballou to his wife, Sarah:

July 14, 1861
Camp Clark

My very dear Sarah:
The indications are very strong that we shall move in a few days—perhaps tomorrow. And lest I should not be able to write you again, I feel impelled to write a few lines that may fall under your eye when I shall be no more. Our movement may be one of a few days' duration and be full of pleasure. And it may be one of severe conflict and death to me. "Not my will but thine O God be done." If it is necessary that I should fall on the battlefield for my Country I am ready. I have no misgivings about, or lack of confidence in, the cause in which I am engaged, and my courage does not halt or falter. I know how strongly American Civilization now leans on the triumph of the Government, and how great a debt we owe to those who went before us through the blood and suffering of the Revolution. And I am willing—perfectly willing—to lay down all my joys in this life, to help maintain this Government, and to pay that debt. . . .

Sarah, my love for you is deathless. It seems to bind me with mighty cables that nothing but Omnipotence could break; and yet my love of Country comes over me like a strong wind and bears me irresistibly on, with all these chains to the battle-field.

The memories of the blissful moments I have enjoyed with you come creeping over me and I feel most deeply grateful to God and to you that I have enjoyed them so long. And how hard it is for me to give them up, and burn to ashes the hopes of future years, when, God willing, we might have lived and loved together, and seen our boys grow up to honorable manhood around us. I know I have but a few small claims upon Providence, but something whispers to me—perhaps it is the wafted prayer of little Edgar, that I shall return to my loved ones unharmed. If I do not, my dear Sarah, never forget how much I love you, nor that when my last breath escapes me on the battle-field, it will whisper your name. . . .

But, O, Sarah, if the dead can come back to this earth and flit unseen around those they loved, I shall be always with you in the gladdest day and in the darkest night, amidst your happiest scene and gloomiest hours— always, always, and if there be a soft breeze upon your cheek, it shall be my breath; or the cool air fans your throbbing temple, it shall be my spirit passing by. Sarah, do not mourn me dead; think I am gone, and wait for me for we shall meet again.

Sullivan

One week after he wrote this letter to his wife, Major Sullivan Ballou of the Second Rhode Island Infantry was killed at the first battle of Bull Run.

This letter clearly reveals why any person would be willing to give his life for his country and to protect the values and the family he holds so dear. I can think of no other reasons that would explain, example after example, why Americans have given their lives to protect such a great heritage as that which we Americans have. May we, of this generation, not easily forget them and still follow their examples of selfless valor!

The War to End All Wars

Let us continue exploring this type of great American heritage as we look at the First World War.

Britain had long dominated the world's seas. France's domination of Continental Europe had been eclipsed by Austria-Hungary and, especially since the Franco-Prussian War thirty years before the turn of the century, by Germany. Everyone seemed to be wary of Germany's emerging industrial and military might, and Germany's Kaiser wasn't satisfied with a mighty army. He wanted a navy that would rival Britain's.

In 1909, Amos S. Hershey, a political science and international law professor at Indiana University, wrote the following in an article for *The Independent*:

> The people of the United States could hardly remain neutral in a war between Germany and Great Britain which might possibly end in German naval supremacy. . . . A blockade of the British Isles by German cruisers and submarine mines, or the loss involved in the danger to contraband trade would be severely felt in this country.
>
> In spite of Hershey's distress about America's potential neutrality, our country managed to do just that—stay neutral—for more than three years of world war. President Wilson desperately wanted to avoid American involvement in the war. He vainly sought to bring

about a negotiated peace between the belligerents. Meanwhile, both sides knew that whichever side could bring the now mighty United States in on its side would almost certainly win the war. (And although there were more American sympathizers for the Allies, the Axis powers also had plenty of American supporters.)

Germany's chancellor clearly saw the danger of any actions that might draw the Americans into the war against Germany and her faltering partners. But Germany's military leaders, like the Kaiser, were enamored of their naval prowess—particularly her submarine U-boats. On January 31, 1917, a dejected German Ambassador Bernstorff reluctantly handed his country's declaration of an unrestricted naval blockade of Britain to U.S. Secretary of State Robert Lansing. From that point forward, Germany declared, any ship, military or merchant, that came near Germany's blockade line would be stopped—by any means necessary.

Three days after Germany's declaration, Wilson severed America's ties with Germany, but he vacillated two more months before declaring war on April 2, 1917. Eighteen months later, Corporal York would come to epitomize America's fighting spirit in this great war. On November 9, 1918, just a few weeks after York's heroics, America had made the difference. The war was over; the Allied forces had won. Oh that the political leaders had shown the courage and strength of determination that its soldiers displayed in the field.

The New World Leader

If there had been any doubts about America's preeminent military and industrial might before World War I, those doubts had vanished by the end of 1918. America was unequivocally the new, world military and economic leader. America's military might had won the war. Now her industrial and agricultural productivity would have to step forward to rebuild much of the rest of the world that had been devastated by the war.

Belgium, lying strategically between Germany and France, had been the first major casualty of World War I. Almost immediately after word of the destruction of Belgium reached the outside world in 1914, forty-year-old Herbert Clark Hoover organized relief efforts for the people of that neutral country. Then, after America's entry into the war, Hoover took over America's Food Administration. So after the war, when much of the world needed American aid to rebuild, Hoover was the logical choice to lead the American Relief Administration. It was no wonder that in a later election, it would be Hoover who would be asked by the leaders of both American political parties to run as president of these United States. He won the election handily.

It is unfortunate and unjust that President Herbert Clark Hoover is often blamed for America's Great Depression. (This unfair treatment will be seen further in chapter 12 as we look at some thoughts that relate to President Hoover's enormous contributions.) He had been in office only ten short months—hardly long enough for his policies to have had much effect—when the stock market crashed. But, without placing blame here, I believe it's sufficient to say that the 1929 stock–market crash was another major turning point in America's history.

A world preoccupied with rebuilding from the destruction of a world war and a worldwide stock–market crash found it easy to overlook the sometimes less-than-subtle signs of military buildup in the fascist countries of Germany, Italy, and Japan. A world longing for peace and prosperity, found it easy to dismiss the aggressive land grabs by these aggressive fascists, until it was too late.

In World War II, America once again tried to stay out of the fighting. Once again, the Axis powers anticipated the danger for them if the United States joined the Allied countries. However, following Japan's gobbling up large parts of Southeast Asia and the Pacific Islands, America froze Japanese financial assets, effectively cutting off Japan's ability to buy the petroleum products it needed to continue its war.

Although Japan's military leaders feared America's entry into the war, they concluded that their best option would be to cripple the US naval fleet with a sudden pre-emptive attack. They did so on the morning of December 7, 1941, Pearl Harbor Day, which according to President Roosevelt was "a day which will live in infamy." On December 8, President Franklin Delano Roosevelt declared war on Japan, and three days later, the United States declared war on Germany and Italy.

The war carried on for four more years. By the time World War II ended, its death and destruction would dwarf that of World War I. The number of casualties still seems unbelievable. Worldwide, more than fifty-five million people died during this war. It was horrendous. It would seem to justify those who say no cause is worth a war. But try telling that to the six million Jews murdered by the Nazis or to the millions of Chinese civilians raped and slaughtered by the Japanese. It was not the bullets and bombs of the war itself that killed most of the people who died during those years. It was the bullets and bombs and starvation caused by ruthless madmen who would have killed even more people had there been no resistance. The war was fought to stop the ruthless murder and enslavement of millions by a few madmen and their duped followers. In a very real sense, it was a war between good and evil.

73

During the war, my father had been assigned to guard General MacArthur's personal residence. Another soldier on the same guard duty told my dad about an important event he had observed while guarding the general.

It was the last night of the general's first stay in the Philippines. The general had arisen from his bed during the middle of the night. This guard could see, and sense, the general's concern. At one point, just before the sun rose, the great general suddenly stopped in front of the window and stared out across the bay.

The soldier remembered that sight when he later heard General MacArthur talking with an officer. The general described to the officer the sight he had seen over the bay from his window that night. There on the horizon, he could see what appeared to him to be angels surrounding the entire Filipino harbor. At that moment, the general felt a confident peace that God had sent His angels to protect the Philippines. He had such a confirmation within him, he believed he would soon return to the Philippines, triumphant over the Japanese forces that were poised to take the islands.

That was the very morning General Douglas MacArthur gave his now world-famous speech, in which he said with an unwavering voice, "I will return." Over the years, Americans would be involved in other wars—declared and undeclared—in which they would distinguish themselves by their courageous self-sacrifices. But to me, no other incident is such a clear example of America's heritage, as time after time, God-fearing men and women experienced a divine protection of this nation and its great principles. We must never forget these sacrifices and values that have made America great and that will keep her great today.

Researching Our
National Disassembly

CHAPTER 5

THE DISASSEMBLY OF
AMERICAN VALUES

In the late '80s and early '90s, there was a quirky and often very funny television series called *Northern Exposure*. The show had brilliant writing and directing. It also had some unwholesome and disturbing plots and language. It had its share of the sexual innuendo that is so common in today's TV fare. But there was one episode that, while it seemed harmless and gentle, was probably more disturbing than any other.

In that episode, the main character, a doctor in remote Alaska, discovered a body perfectly preserved in ice. The body clearly had been entombed in the ice for a long time. In fact, the astute doctor began to suspect that the body just might be that of the famous Napoleon Bonaparte. He quietly had some tests done—without revealing the details of his discovery—and confirmed that there was substantial evidence that the frozen body very well could be that of the famous French conqueror.

The doctor initially confided his discovery with just one close friend, a practitioner of New Age philosophies. Together, the two of them discussed how Napoleon might have wound up frozen in Alaska, and the implications of such a discovery. The implications were serious, indeed.

Perhaps, the doctor postulated, history as we learned it, is wrong and needs to be corrected. The doctor, a man of science, was ready to break the news and let the chips fall where they may. But the doctor's New Age friend persuaded him otherwise. History, the friend convinced the doctor, is not about what we know, but about what we choose to believe. Why risk everything we've come to believe? In the end, the friend persuaded the doctor that his desire for truth based on facts was selfish and unnecessary. Belief won out over fact. The world was spared, in the opinion of this television character, the trouble of revising history, in spite of contrary facts.

A Dangerous Disregard for Truth

The *Northern Exposure* episode was a problem for two reasons. The first problem was its apparent espousal of belief over fact.[8] The second problem was the ironic spin. In that show, history, as we all know it, was wrong but was allowed to go unchallenged by the facts in order to preserve and protect our long-cherished beliefs.

I call the second problem ironic because the choice to disregard the truth was made to avoid rewriting a long-held, and apparently firmly established, episode in history. The far more common scenario these days is ignoring firmly established historical facts in favor of a "different history," revised by one or another pushy, special-interest group and forced on the rest of society in the name of egalitarianism.

Mary Lefkowitz, observed Andrew M. Mellon Professor in the Humanities at Wellesley College, wrote the following to explain why she wrote a book titled *Not Out of Africa*:

> Normally, if one has a question about a text that another instructor is using, one simply asks why he or she is using that book. But since the conventional line of

inquiry was closed to me, I had to wait till I could raise my questions in a more public context. That opportunity came in February 1993, when Dr. Yosef A. A. ben-Jochannan was invited to give Wellesley's Martin Luther King Jr. memorial lecture. Posters described Dr. ben-Jochannan as a "distinguished Egyptologist," and indeed that is how he was introduced by the then President of Wellesley College. But I knew from my research in Afrocentric literature that he was not what scholars would ordinarily describe as an Egyptologist, that is a scholar of Egyptian language and civilization. Rather, he was an extreme Afrocentrist, author of many books describing how Greek civilization was stolen from Africa, how Aristotle robbed the library of Alexandria, and how the true Jews are Africans like himself.

Lefkowitz goes on to explain that Dr. ben-Jochannan made the same claims during his speech at Wellesley. During the question-and-answer period that followed the speech, she asked the doctor why he would claim that Aristotle had gone to Egypt with Alexander and stolen his philosophy from the library at Alexandria, when that library was built twenty-five years after Aristotle's death. Dr. ben-Jochannan gave no answer; he simply said that he "resented the tone of the inquiry." After the lecture, several students went to Dr. Lefkowitz and called her a racist.

Dr. William Durden, executive director of the Institute for the Academic Advancement of Youth at Johns Hopkins University, wrote an article for *Wisconsin Interest* magazine that told of some of the same chilling disregard for truth. He began the article by telling the story of his experience as a member of a task force "charged with making recommendations to improve the status of gifted and talented students in a large, East Coast, urban school system."

The school system was in dismal shape. It seemed, however, that the superintendent and assistant superintendent already had their view on the key to the solution. (Now understand that this was a grossly underachieving school district with a huge dropout rate and entire high schools from which not one student would take a College Board Advanced Placement exam.) The key to solving the problem, according to the superintendent and his assistant? Require all students to take calculus. Their reasoning was ". . . the United States is the only highly industrialized nation in which calculus is not required of its high-school graduates."

It might have been a reasonable demand, if the assertion had been based on facts. When Dr. Durden presented verifiable facts in writing, refuting those assertions from several other industrialized countries, the superintendent and assistant simply ignored them. In fact at the next meeting, the assistant superintendent, who was running the meeting, reasserted his position about calculus, stating that the facts were "irrelevant and superfluous."

In his article, Durden then goes on to trace such disregard for facts to postmodernism. Postmodernism is, essentially, a reaction to the modernistic school of thought that grew out of the Enlightenment. As a result of the Enlightenment, many "forward thinkers" began to assume that rational man, free from his age-old "religious superstitions," would be able to gain unlimited knowledge that would solve all man's problems.

Before too long, other thinkers began to see that modernism wasn't working. Knowledge alone was not going to save mankind from his own demons and the often cruel ways of the world. Those thinkers reacted to modernism by developing their own new philosophy that had more in common with Eastern mysticism than with Western rationalism. The result was a postmodern worldview that sees knowledge as fanciful, and that truth is in the eye (or mind) of the beholder.

According to historian Gertrude Himmelfarb, the effect of postmodernism on history and on the teaching of history, has been "a *denial* of the fixity of the past, of the reality of the past apart from what the historian chooses to make of it, and thus *of any objective truth about the past*" (italics added).

People or Principles?

Chapter 1 of this book dealt with the founding of this country and the values that led to, and emanated, from those events. The trend in today's educational environment would deem those events to be less important than the lessons learned and beliefs gained from them, as though the beliefs can be divorced from the events. And if those carefully re-corded events disturb our belief systems, then the politi-cally correct crowd will move the focus of history away from them and onto events that support their beliefs or else rewrite them to support those beliefs.

Many believe that this is among the purposes of the federal government's Goals 2000. The provisions of the National Education Goals (Goals 2000) sound reasonable. Those provisions outline the following:

1. School readiness
2. School completion
3. Student achievement and citizenship
4. Teacher education and professional development
5. Mathematics and science
6. Adult literacy and lifelong learning
7. Safe, disciplined, and alcohol- and drug-free schools
8. Parental participation

So what's wrong? These things sound great. But some who have dug a bit deeper find some less-than-pure motives and less-than-ideal results.

Phillip C. Clarke, who writes a syndicated column titled "Behind the Headlines," wrote the following about America's new education goals:

> Consider what Lynne Cheney reported recently in the *Wall Street Journal*. Cheney, former head of the National Endowment for the Humanities, reviewed the proposed [Goals 2000 education] standards for teaching history, and stated simply, they are appalling. In 31 standards, for example, the Constitution is not even mentioned. . . .
>
> Cheney also notes that "counting how many times different subjects are mentioned in the document yields telling results." For instance, Paul Revere, Alexander Graham Bell, Thomas Edison, Albert Einstein, Jonas Salk and the Wright Brothers are not mentioned at all in the history teaching standards. But the American Federation of Labor gets nine mentions. . . .

It's a clear case of revisionist history. And it's a blatant violation of the Constitution, the document that our founders established to protect our freedoms—and that the Goals 2000 document so carefully ignores.

In Lake County, Florida, the America-First curriculum guidelines approved by the local school board, quickly came under attack from the politically correct crowd. Those guidelines, established at the *local level* (and remember, the Constitution was written specifically to allow such decisions to remain at the *local level*), call for "instill[ing] in our students an appreciation of our American heritage and culture, such as: our republican form of government, capitalism, a free-enterprise system, patriotism, strong family values, freedom of religion and other basic values. . . ."

In response to the local school board's decision, the "education director"[9] for the group, People for the American Way, called the policy "basically a hate campaign for kids." Another commentator Michael Kinsley called the curriculum "garbage." Not surprisingly, the Florida Education Association filed a lawsuit against the school board and its American heritage curriculum. In all sincerity, some of the attackers viewed the curriculum as having the potential to cause a divisive and arrogant sense of superiority in the students with whom it would be used. But Pat Hart, chair of the Lake County school board, responded, "It is not who we are that is superior; it's what we stand for."

And that—"what we stand for"—truly is the strength of a great nation. America has remained strong for two centuries because we have been "a nation of laws and not of men" founded on a clear set of moral principles (as already identified in chapter 1). We have survived and prospered despite the blunders, foibles, and sometimes the outright deceit of some of our leaders, because we have fundamentally been guided, not by those men and women, but by a set of principles and laws established by our founders, based on God's principles and laws as revealed in the Bible. James Madison, the man most responsible for the drafting of the Constitution, wrote, "We have staked the whole of our political institutions on the capacity of mankind to govern themselves according to the Ten Commandments of God."

Many believe, however, that Madison's reasoning was somewhat flawed in that, on his own, no one is able to govern himself (perfectly) according to God's Ten Commandments. But ours is a world of two kingdoms—God's kingdom and the world's kingdom. Some of us have chosen to join God's kingdom, but as long as we're alive on this earth, none of us can escape the world's kingdom. Our collective lives within the world's kingdom is society. Society is made up of individuals, often with conflicting views and wants. So society must be governed. Society can be governed by people or by principle. Our founders saw the wisdom of the latter.

Our society, particularly in the last fifty years, has been dismantling the Constitution, discrediting the moral principles, and moving toward a government based on people rather than on principles and laws. The chief vehicle used in this move has been, and is, our education system.

Egalitarian Education

If you are a parent of school-age children (for that matter, if you are an adult living anywhere in the United States), you probably at least have heard the term *outcome-based education* (OBE). The program has been a center of controversy for years. It has been praised as the salvation of our school systems and vilified as a chief instrument in an elitist goal for world domination.

Here's a simple definition of OBE: "OBE is simply the establishment of expected goals or outcomes for different levels of elementary-secondary education, and a commitment to ensuring that every student achieves at least those minimum proficiencies before being allowed to graduate."[10]

"Outcomes are *measurable* results of learning," according to OBE theorists William Spady and Kit Marshall. It sounds reasonable and nonthreatening. And it certainly seems simple enough. Under this system, teachers make a target, or an "outcome," (hence the name of the program) for all the students to achieve. When a student reaches that target (outcome) he is given the next target.

When he reaches all his targets, his education is complete. Those who do not hit the target on the first try get another try, and another, and another, and as many as needed to hit it. Eventually everyone "achieves." What a great way to build self-esteem—everyone wins; no one fails. And don't the educators look good in the process?

But the very important questions are (or at least should be): "What are the children learning?" and "What is the target chosen to achieve?"

The very sad answer seems to be, "Not much." A 1987 Johns Hopkins University study of "Mastery Learning" (a standard OBE teaching method) labeled the program "a Robin Hood approach to learning" that focuses on repetitive teaching for low achievers at the expense of high achievers. A 1988 survey in Minnesota schools that use outcome-based education discovered that 55 percent of class time was spent on nonacademic subjects. Again, the problem seemed to be that the system focused on the low achievers, consequently diminishing or negating motivation for high achievers.

According to Harold W. Stevenson, a professor of psychology at the University of Michigan, and as reported in the April 13, 1993, issue of *The Washington Post*, "In Asia, you are defying the norm by not doing well [in school]. . . . In America, you are defying the norm by doing well." What a sad commentary to think that the norm for education in America has become failure or low achievement. Despite many such findings, outcome-based education continues to be brought into more schools. Help us as parents and concerned Americans to be prepared to participate in processes (as will be spelled out in chapter 12), which will encourage a restoration to the norm of doing well as a student.

And what happens when parents—the *most* local level of government—object to such teaching methods? According to a 1991 report by a bipartisan select committee appointed by Michigan's state legislature, the top officials in the Department of Education and Public Health had recommended that "any parent or teacher who got in the way of implementing the Michigan Model [of OBE] was to be labeled as a right-wing, fundamentalist Christian fanatic." Is this an example of government by the people and based on principles as expressed by our founding fathers?

The Sinister Side of OBE

This heavy-handed censorship of any opposition points to the more sinister aspects of OBE, extending as far back as 1972 when Chester M. Pierce, in his keynote address to the Association for Childhood Education, stated the following:

> Every child in America entering school at the age of five is insane because he comes to school with certain allegiances toward our founding fathers, toward his parents, toward a belief in a supernatural being. . . . It's up to you, teachers, to make all of these sick children well by creating the international children of the future.[11]

Does this imply that those young men who were dying for their country on the battlefront in Southeast Asia at this time were grownup "sick children"? How ironic that Mr. Pierce's OBE philosophy did not seem to object to others dying to protect them, the generations of American heroes of our armed forces who have given their lives to protect his right to make such a sick comment.

Many see OBE as one key tool in the globalists' arsenal aimed at bringing a whole generation into subjection and subservience. The purpose of OBE is to teach "global values" rather than verifiable facts—especially facts that engender national allegiance. Dr. Shirley McCune of Midwest Regional Laboratories stated in a speech at the 1989 Governors Conference on Education, "[What] we have to do is to build a future. . . . in curriculum . . . [where] *we no longer are teaching facts to children*" (italics added).

The January 3, 1996 issue of *The Detroit News* ran an article that featured one Detroit couple's decision to pull their daughter out of an OBE public school. The article, titled "Lines are drawn over outcome-based education" said, "The final straw for Tim and Betsy French was a class project. Their daughter, a third-grader, was told to describe in writing a crime she thought of committing and then fingerprint herself." The Frenches had had enough. They, like a growing number of parents, took their daughter out of the public school and enrolled her in a private school. (Do we wonder why students plan and carry out acts of aggression and murder against fellow students and school faculties? Are they, in part, mimicking what some teacher has given them to do as a school project?)

The article continued: "Dr. Alan Coulson, a California psychologist, pioneered 'non-directive' education, which later became the foundation for OBE, in the 1960s with colleague Dr. Carl Rogers. The two men speculated that allowing children to develop in the classroom at their own pace would leave crucial time for them to 'figure things out for themselves.'"

Coulson today travels the world retracting what he and Rogers produced in a series of textbooks, *Studies of the Person*.

"Allow children to work at their own pace," said Coulson. ". . . and they just drift when they're not held on task. When an experiment fails, you stop. And this experiment has failed."

In an effort to move the philosophy of OBE beyond the classroom, other efforts are being made. At the time of this writing, pending legislation (House Resolution 6) would establish a national school board. House Resolution 1617 would create a national electronic database as part of a "national labor market information system" that would collect personal and psychological information on all people in the work force. It also would reclassify sixteen year olds as adults in order to avoid child labor laws, allowing them to be put to work in apprenticeship programs instead of finishing their last two years of high school.

Some, including noted Christian author Berit Kjos, see clear parallels between OBE and the Nazis' manipulation of education to indoctrinate German youth. In her book, *Brave New Schools*, she examines some of those parallels. Kjos quoted the following from a book by J. Noakes and G. Pridham titled *Nazism: A History in Documents and Eyewitness Accounts, 1919–1945*: "The Nazi leadership appreciated the difficulty of indoctrinating the older generation. . . . They were all the more determined to mold the new generation along Nazi lines. As the leader of the Nazi Teacher's League, Hans Schemm, put it: 'Those who have the youth on their side control the future.'"

Right here in my home state of Oregon, the so-called "Oregon Option" puts this state at the forefront of those "brave new schools."

On December 5, 1994, the entire Clinton cabinet, along with all the members of the Oregon congressional delegation—outgoing Governor Barbara Roberts; newly elected Governor John Kitzhaber; Portland Mayor Vera Katz; and other notable locals—signed a document called "The Oregon Option." Vice President Al Gore said the plan would turn the state into a laboratory.

The Oregon Option will set up databases on every child conceived in the state. Government social workers will then make regular home visits to evaluate the parents and their homes to determine if they meet state-established standards. Failure to abide by the program will be labeled "developmental neglect" and will be considered grounds for the government to take away the child from its home and parents.

In 1991, the then Speaker of the Oregon House, Vera Katz, sponsored HB 3565 (Oregon Twenty-First-Century Education Act). Her bill was based on the research of a private group called the National Center on Education and the Economy (NCEE). The group included some of the country's most influential people from government and big business. Their goal was to redesign the nation's education system.

Two of the relatively less notables (at that time) among that group of movers and shakers were Oregon's House Speaker, and the wife of the governor of Arkansas—one Hillary Rodham Clinton.

(By the way, Vera Katz was the only elected official appointed to President Clinton's National Skills Standards Board—the very body that oversaw the development of the national plan for outcome-based education, known as Goals 2000.)

It seems clear to those who look beneath the surface, that there is a dangerous trend in moving away from a fact-based educational system to one of global indoctrination. It is that very globalistic mindset that finds the teaching of historical facts about our nation (especially about the values of our founders as stated in and protected by our Declaration of Independence and Constitution) so detestable.

For the sake of our country and our children, we must never let future generations forget the freedoms won for them by their forebears and by the documents that have preserved those freedoms and held us together for two centuries.

There are two principles that education must never forget. The first is that true education is building a foundation on past achievements with a challenge to replicate the best of the past in the lives of future generations. This is especially true in America. When we teach our American children the heritage of our past, we are helping them understand their own identity. One reason that we have such a level of frustration and anger in our young people today is because they have lost sight of who they are and where they have come from.

This loss leads into the second basic principle: When each American is recognized as unique, special, important, and of worth, then and only then is America a great nation. When the greatness of each individual American is esteemed, encouraged, and held high, the concept of a government of the people, by the people, and for the people has profound significance. Today's American students have been robbed of this understanding. When children are not taught that they were created by an entity who had a plan when creating the universe and each individual, then there can be no sense of worth or identity as an individual. This is why our errant education structure of today stifles individual achievement under the guise of benefiting the majority of students.

We need to return education in America to the basics. Teach students about their self-worth as supported by our heritage and by their being a special creation. Second, we need to restore an unalterable system of preserving a basic course of study of our American heritage that will be constant in core content. In short, we should not allow today's professional educators to be experimenting with the minds and lives of our national heritage and future—our youth.

CHAPTER 6

THE DISASSEMBLY
OF PERSONAL ACHIEVEMENT

Let no debt remain outstanding, except the continuing debt to love one another, for he who loves his fellow-man has fulfilled the law. (Rom. 13:8)

A little boy and his grandmother were taking a walk in the woods one afternoon when suddenly the child stopped. "Look, Grandma," he called, staring in wonder at a fallen twig.

"What is it?" his grandmother asked, stepping over to join him. The little boy pointed at the small white cocoon glistening in the afternoon sun. The cocoon was attached to the fallen twig, and as they stared, it began to move. Before long the hard white shell of the cocoon burst open, and a small black form began to emerge.

The boy's eyes grew as wide as silver dollars as he watched the tiny creature's struggle.

"What's the matter, Grandma?" he asked. "What's wrong with this little animal?"

"It's a butterfly," Grandma explained. "There's nothing wrong with it, honey. God has provided the butterfly with this hard cocoon to protect it and to help it grow strong as it struggles to get free."

"But can't we help?" the little boy asked. "He's having such a hard time."

The grandmother shook her head. "No," she said, "if we try to help, we'll be interfering with its natural process. The butterfly needs to struggle to develop its strength. Otherwise, it won't be able to fly away, and soon it will die."

The little boy continued to watch, his face grimacing as if he felt the butterfly's pain; his fingers twitching with his desire to reach out and help. Finally, both wings emerged from the cocoon and opened to their full extent. The boy gasped as the sunlight caught the brilliant purples, yellows, and blues of the butterfly's wings. The boy was awestruck. "Isn't it beautiful?" he whispered.

The grandmother nodded. "It certainly is," she agreed. "And if we wait just a little longer, we'll see it fly off into the sky."

Well-Meaning Mistakes

Just as this example is true in nature, and specifically in the life of a monarch butterfly, it is even more applicable to people. So often, when we see people struggling to get free of a situation, we, much like the little boy, find ourselves grimacing, our fingers twitching with the desire to reach out and help. Sometimes that is exactly what we need to do. But more often than not, we can cause more harm than good by our interference. Just as the butterfly needs to struggle to force life giving fluid into its wings and body so must people sometimes struggle. This allows them to take control of their own solutions and build self-esteem which comes from personal achievement.

In America today, many of us try to help others in ways that make us feel good, giving us an instant sense of satisfaction for having assisted a needy person. Americans are known for their generosity in giving money, food, clothing, and other gifts; but we are often sadly deficient in giving time to actually listen to and interact with those in need. This very penchant for giving "things" has been the primary motive for establishing many of the governmental programs in place today.

Our welfare program, for example, was birthed by a group of well-meaning Americans, seeking to meet the needs of the less fortunate in our society. Sadly, those who established this program chose to address the problems from a distance, rather than from a one-on-one evaluation of the need of the individual or family. As a result, a system designed to provide for the emergency needs of those who go through difficult times in their lives, has turned into a system that limits personal growth and incentive, while at the same time promotes slavery to governmental handouts. In reality, these well-intentioned programs hinder the necessary development and maturity of the very individuals they were intended to help.

By preventing people from developing basic problem-solving skills, many of our assistance and entitlement programs teach them that they ought to expect the government and others to take responsibility for their problems. The resulting frustration is often vented against family members, fellow workers, and society in general through rage, abuse, and other destructive acts.

To break this destructive cycle of dependency, we need to return to developing programs geared toward assisting people to find practical solutions to their individual problems. We need to allow people the privilege and freedom of finding their own solutions, absent of the government imposing its solutions on them. People deserve the right to exercise this freedom apart from governmentally created enticements.

Government would better serve needy people if it functioned as a resource to finding solutions, rather than inhibiting individuals from following the step-by-step process necessary to finding their own solutions to the problems of life. The democratic government was never meant to be a "big brother," spying on the personal affairs of its citizens; neither was it meant to be a doting parent, catering to its children's every whim or desire, without first giving them the opportunity to learn how to deal with their own problems and find their own solutions.

Suggested Solutions

The Trust Note program, which I am proposing in a later chapter of this book, would help give Americans many incentives to become working, tax-paying citizens. Unfortunately, the government today has offered a larger number of incentives not to work than it has to be gainfully employed. We would do well to heed the advice of Captain John Smith, governor of the Jamestown Virginia Colony in 1608, who when he found that many people were neglecting their day-to-day duties and allowing others to carry a double share of the burden, established a law based on 2 Thessalonians 3:10: "He that will not work shall not eat." In a colony of 150 people, Smith found that only thirty or forty colonists were doing all the work. In addition, he found that those who did work were spending only six hours daily in work, and the rest was spent in "pastime and merry exercises."[12]

We need to reestablish a John Smith-type of work-ethic policy today to help Americans develop a sense of ownership and self-pride, which will encourage them to want to work and become contributing, tax-paying citizens.

One program that could be developed along these lines is a needs-assessment and community resource guide that would catalog job assistance, community help, and counseling resources of the community. This would allow the widest exposure of all the available community resources to persons needing specific kinds of assistance. These companies, volunteers, and organizations could be assisted in making their resources available to those who could best use them. The government could simply facilitate this process by maintaining a resource database on a regional and national basis, accessible through libraries, community agency offices, the Internet, local churches, service organizations, and various other means.

Another solution would be to develop publicly funded work training programs to help people get into the workplace, while at the same time, help them discover and develop their unique gifts and talents. The government could offer partial pay or special tax incentives to certain companies or community organizations that would then provide jobs and training to people who are in need of career-change services. These could be construction projects for developing modern public transportation or apprentice-type programs to perpetuate skills that are needed and valuable to our society. This could also be used for programs that have work-experience restrictions, which make it difficult for people to enter these trades due to the low wages offered.

I am confident that if government took a back seat in the process of helping others, those who have a calling and practical experience in various areas would come to the forefront with the right ideas and encouragement. This is one example of a way in which where Americans would continue to show the practical compassion that comes from unity. Americans need opportunities to share their callings, gifts, and talents to help others fulfill their personal dreams. We show the best of America's greatness when each one of us is given the chance to encourage and help others develop and pursue their dreams through the sharing of our own lives and dreams.

As Bill Bradley, former United States Senator and former New York Knicks basketball player, says, "If we are ever to move toward racial harmony in America, we must seize every opportunity for . . . cooperation. Only through doing things together—things that have nothing specifically to do with race—will people break down racial barriers. Facing common problems as neighbors or coworkers reduces awkwardness in a way that simple conversation cannot."[13]

Uniting individual Americans to face our common problems together—such as balancing the budget, paying off the national debt, preserving programs to help the elderly, and reducing welfare roles and crime rates—is much more effective than trying to put bandages on these problems through governmental bailout programs.

Americans are givers. They want to help their fellow man, and they need to be given opportunities to work together, so as to help others on a more personal level, rather than simply paying taxes to the government, so the government can, in turn, subsidize a never-ending cycle of poverty and despair.

Positive Examples

Although there are countless examples in our history of men and women who exemplified this type of selfless, giving American, one of the most recent and notable examples is Martin Luther King Jr. His famous "I Have a

Dream" speech has become a part of the courageous and beautiful tapestry of our country's history. A man committed to nonviolence, King did as much, or more, than any other individual to further the rights and better the lives of everyone in our society, regardless of race, creed, or social status. Yet he was also a man who inspired people to develop and use their talents and gifts to climb out of their "victim mentality" and become victors. He was a model of hard work and dedication, a leader who called people to fulfill their potential and to set a higher standard for their children and their children's children.

Chosen in January 1964 by *Time* magazine as Man of the Year, King also became the youngest recipient of the Nobel Peace Prize later that year. He was a man who faced incredible odds and violent opposition, but he did not back down nor compromise his convictions. As a result, he impacted and changed countless lives as he led by example. His legacy as a man of peace and courage continues, although his life was snuffed out by an assassin's bullet in 1968.

Although few will ever gain the notoriety of Martin Luther King Jr., there are countless unsung heroes like him throughout our great land, people who lead by example and give of themselves to others on a regular basis. And there are many more who would rise to the challenge to do the same if the opportunities were available to them.

Lynn Carr of St. Charles, Missouri, is a perfect example. In 1984 she lost her job and her home. She and her five-year-old son lived in their car for one week, until it was repossessed. They then moved from one friend's house to another, seeking a way out of their situation.

In the midst of all this, Lynn decided to go back to school and work toward achieving a high-school equivalency diploma. She also spent a lot of time baking and listening to self-help tapes. Through her baking, she developed several new recipes for cheesecakes. When she took her cakes to different restaurants and offered them for sale, they sold out almost immediately.

In time, Lynn met a man at church, and they were married. Before long, she was selling cheesecakes from her home. Later, she opened Twain-land Cheesecake Company and Café in Hannibal. Success came quickly, and Lynn decided to use her recent experiences to help others in similar situations.

Hiring only welfare moms or high-school dropouts, Lynn encourages her employees through the use of motivational videos. She also plans to expand her company and incorporate a learning center and a day-care center, enabling her employees to use part of the workday to study for high-school equivalency diplomas.[14]

Dorothy Balsis Thompson is a former TV-commercial producer who thinks that with the right opportunities and guidance, anyone from any walk of life can be a success. As part of the show-business industry, Dorothy felt that her profession wasn't doing enough to help young people from the inner city. So in May 1992, she founded a nonprofit organization called Streetlight Production Assistant Program. The program recruits former gang members, ex-convicts, high-school dropouts, and people on welfare, and then trains them for entry-level positions in the entertainment industry. Although it took all of Dorothy's time, savings, and persistence to convince those within the industry to hire her graduates, the program has been a success. Many of those who seemed to have no future other than the streets, prisons, or welfare roles, are now actively employed doing films, TV shows, and commercials.[15]

Robin Williams (not the actor) is number five of six sisters. Her four older sisters were all teenage mothers, but Robin did not follow in their footsteps. While in high school, Robin joined Best Friends, a program established in 1987 by Elayne Bennett, whose husband, William J. Bennett, was the Education Secretary at the time. The goals of Best Friends is to equip young girls with the self-respect necessary to say no to detrimental influences, such as teen sex and drug use, and to adopt positive practices and goals, such as proper nutrition, physical fitness, and successful careers.

Best Friends' success was measured by a poll taken in 1995 by David Rowberry, a doctoral student at the University of Colorado at Boulder. Results showed that 66 percent of girls in Washington's public school system had experienced sex by the time they were in the twelfth grade, as compared to 10 percent of Best Friends members. The teenage-pregnancy rate was 22 percent for those in the public schools and 1 percent for those belonging to Best Friends.

Robin was not one of the 1 percent. She now has a successful gospel-singing career, having released her first album when she was sixteen. She also goes back to her old high school to encourage current Best Friends members to maintain their self-respect and not settle for anything less than the best.[16]

Not only did Lynn Carr find success through her own struggles, she then turned around and offered her experience to help and encourage others, as did Robin Williams. Dorothy Balsis Thompson gave of herself by offering her experience and expertise to inspire hope in many who considered themselves hopeless. How many untapped resources like Lynn Carr, Robin Williams, and Dorothy Balsis Thompson are out there, ready and available to give of themselves, to offer their assistance, and to mentor others? And how many who are now trapped in a dead-end welfare system or the revolving doors of prison life would be happier and more fulfilled by receiving help from one of those mentors, instead of continuing to rely on the charity of the government or the forced assistance of penal institutions?

And what about Lynn's son or the girls influenced by Robin's visits to Best Friends? How much better chance do they have for a bright future than if Lynn or Robin had succumbed to the victim mentality that has trapped so many in the generational cycle of welfare and poverty? Like Martin Luther King Jr., these women each had a dream. Through struggle, hard work, and determination, they saw those dreams fulfilled—and influenced others to pursue their own dreams as well.

The freedom that is America was birthed as a dream in the lives of so many Americans. We cannot allow the impotency of our impersonal, governmental assistance programs to continue to steal that dream and turn it into a nightmare for future generations of America's potential heroes. In chapters 9 through 12, I will explore how we can help keep those dreams alive.

CHAPTER 7

THE DISASSEMBLY OF GOVERNMENTAL ACCOUNTABILITY

Duty. Honor. Country. Those three hallowed words reverently dictate what you ought to be, what you can be, what you will be. They are the rallying points, to build courage when courage seems to fail, to regain faith when there seems to be little cause for faith, to create hope when hope becomes forlorn. . . .

—General Douglas MacArthur
West Point, May 12, 1962

Looking at the early history of America, we saw example after example of how our founding fathers were willing to sacrifice their personal lives, their wealth, and their liberty for the establishment and preservation of this great nation. We would like to think that, as the country matured and developed a new philosophy, these examples of self-sacrifice also would grow and abound in our system of government. Unfortunately, I believe our modern-day examples of government can be summed up in this statement: A government sworn to protect itself at all cost, even by extracting sacrifices of its people to maintain its growing bureaucracy.

To paraphrase the words of former President Kennedy, one could say that today our government tells Americans they are called not to ask what the government can do for them, but what they can give to preserve the government. Today's government is a far cry from the founding glory of a government "of the people, by the people, and for the people."

We can see many examples of how the government has slowly changed to a self-preservation mentality at the expense of America's great citizens. One such example in recent times is that of General Douglas MacArthur. For MacArthur, the principles of duty, honor, and country would be the guiding beacons throughout his life—in spite of his government's eventual betrayal of him and those same principles.

That betrayal began in 1950, when President Harry S. Truman became the first American president to send American troops to fight in an undeclared war. When the United Nations Security Council called for member nations to intervene in the hostilities that were breaking out as the communist North Koreans were invading South Korea, Truman circumvented the Constitution—which states that Congress must approve a declaration of war—by calling for a "policing action." Regardless of his motives, and whether or not the cause was just, Harry S. Truman, the president of the United States had defied the Constitution he had sworn to uphold.

Then, to make matters worse, Truman dismissed MacArthur as the leader of the American forces in Korea. (Although the official line was that MacArthur was relieved of his command because he disobeyed orders, many believe that the real reason he was sent packing was because he was winning the undeclared war, and a quick American victory was not part of the plan. If you want to know more about this theory, read *Changing Commands: The Betrayal of America's Military*, by John F. McManus.)

Although the "policing action" ended with a truce agreement in 1953, America's fighting forces could not claim the victories their predecessors had won in previous wars. But the biggest losers were the American people, whose hard-won and long-protected Constitution had suffered a grave assault, and not from an external enemy.

When the Servant Seeks to Become Master

Truman's action of circumventing the Constitution in the Korean "conflict" probably wasn't the first, and certainly wouldn't be the only, violation of the Constitution by an American president. Most of the other violations, like Truman's, probably were by well-meaning men who had concluded that the end justified the means. But remember, our founders set up a nation of laws and not of men. For our country to maintain the liberty envisioned by the framers of the Constitution, the principles of that Constitution must outweigh the whims, no matter how wise or well-intentioned any individual or group is.

Our founders knew the dangers of too much power in the hands of one individual or one group. That's why they devised a three-part federal government that would allow for checks and balances. That's also why they called for most decisions to be made at the state and local level. They forged a United States government that would be "of the people, by the people, and for the people." The government would be in place to serve the people. The people were never to be tools in service of the government, and the chief instrument to protect the relationship of the people with the government is the Constitution. That's why it's such a grave matter when those who are sworn to uphold the Constitution not only fail to uphold it, but blatantly defy it.

Lord Acton stated it best when he said, "Power corrupts, and absolute power corrupts absolutely." There must be tremendous temptations for those in high-level government positions to misuse the power of government. And sadly, when average citizens see the all-too-frequent examples of those misuses and abuses, we have a tendency to become cynical and to want to separate ourselves from such behavior. Many citizens then choose to disconnect altogether from the political process—even to the point of not voting. Then, perhaps in part because of public apathy, politicians continue in an ever-growing way to take unto themselves duties that rightly belong to the people. The process becomes a vicious cycle, and government turns into an unresponsive monster that feeds on everything around it for self-preservation.

The Original Intent

James Madison, our fourth president and one of our nation's founders and primary author of the Constitution, wrote the following: "In framing a government which is to be administered by men over men, the great difficulty lies in this: you must first enable the government to control the governed; and in the next place *oblige it to govern itself*" (emphasis added).

Madison also wrote in "Federalist Paper #45":

> The powers delegated by the proposed Constitution to the federal government are few and defined. Those which are to remain in the State governments are numerous

and indefinite. The former will be exercised principally on external objects, as war, peace, negotiation, and foreign commerce. . . . The powers reserved to the several states will extend to all the objects which, in the ordinary course of affairs, concern the lives, liberties, and properties of the people, and the internal order, improvement, and prosperity of the State.

Our founding fathers and early leaders saw their leadership as a public service, subject to the people, that was to be rendered for a time, after which they would return to their private lives and turn over the reigns of leadership to other temporary public servants. In those times, no one ever sought to make a career of political leadership. But contrast that principle of temporary service to the public by patriotic citizens, against today's career politicians whose retirement pensions exceed the income of the average working American.

Government was intended to be a minimal part of our lives. The intent was that government would protect our lives, our properties, and our freedoms—not extract from them the price to build its control over them. Clearly, James Madison and the framers of the Constitution wanted to guard against a bloated, self-serving federal government. But over the decades, less honorable leaders have gradually eroded the protections against government growth and intrusion that our founders had so carefully built. For many career politicians and their followers, government has become an end rather than a means.

Erosion and Perversion of the Original Intent

In our day, many of us—even among conservative-leaning, middle Americans—have become so accustomed to government's intrusion into our lives and our income, that we take it for granted. We forget—or were never aware—that today's massive government is a relatively new phenomenon. But think about this: No generation prior to that of your grandparents or great-grandparents (depending on your age) ever had to deal with a government that so infringed upon their privacy. They never had to deal with any of the following intrusions that are now a part of our daily lives:

- Sales taxes
- Income taxes
- Social Security taxes
- National Labor Relations Board
- Equal Employment Opportunity Commission
- Interstate Commerce Commission
- Federal Trade Commission
- Farm subsidies
- Price supports
- And a host of others

"Yes," many would argue, "but what about the need to deal with crooked businessmen and neighbors, as well as the whims of devastating natural forces? That's why these government agencies, supports, and taxes became necessary—to protect the little guy."

That argument of "protecting the little guy" is not altogether without merit. But one can argue with equal or greater validity this question: "Who is best suited to protect the little guy?" And perhaps even more importantly, "What protections for the little guy are appropriate?"

Yes, our elderly citizens who have worked long and hard for most of their lives should be able to retire in their golden years without fear of poverty. Certainly, our children should be given the best possible education to help them become not just productive, but also honest and honorable members of society. Surely, businesses should not be allowed to take unfair advantage of their employees.

But should massive, inefficient, and often very partisan federal agencies be allowed to regulate small businesses out of business? Are there better ways of "protecting the little guy"? Can those who truly need protection get that protection without the cost of government encroachment into the lives and finances of everyday citizens? I believe so, and we will look at some answers to some of those questions in later chapters. But first let's examine the problem a little more closely.

To get a better picture of this phenomenon of government growth and intrusion, let's look at some numbers. As late as the early years of this century, government spending as a percentage of the gross national product (GNP) was just 7 percent or less. Allowing for the expected increases for war expenditures, we see that following World War I, that figure had risen to more than 10 percent. It then hit a plateau of about 20 percent during the late thirties. Then, of course, there was another huge increase to cover the costs of World War II, after which the figure dropped in the years following the war. Then, from about 1950 to the present, the government's spending percentage of the GNP has increased steadily, so that the 1996 figure was 30.6 percent.[17] That's more than a fourfold increase in the government's take of our nation's productivity this century!

Our desire for justice, equality, and security (brought to us by way of a benevolent government) has taken us to places our founding fathers never intended and where many of us know we shouldn't be. Here's Milton and Rose

Friedman's (Nobel Prize-winning economists) take on how we got here:

> Ironically, the very success of economic and political freedom reduced its appeal to later thinkers. The narrowly limited government of the late nineteenth century possessed little concentrated power that endangered the ordinary man. The other side of that coin was that it possessed little power that would enable people to do good. And in an imperfect world there were still many evils. Indeed, the very progress of society made the residual evils seem all the more objectionable. As always, people took the favorable developments for granted. They forgot the danger to freedom from a strong government. Instead, they were attracted by the good that a stronger government could achieve—if only government power were in the "right" hands. . . .
>
> Emphasis on the responsibility of the individual for his own fate was replaced by emphasis on the individual as a pawn buffeted by forces beyond his control. The view that government's role is to serve as an umpire to prevent individuals from coercing one another was replaced by the view that government's role is to serve as a parent charged with the duty of coercing some to aid others.[18]

As we have seen, the beginnings of the government growth process had started even before the Great Depression of the late 1920s and early 1930s. The huge jumps occurred as a result of the Roosevelt administration's attempts to reverse the economic effects of the Great Depression. A well-intentioned Roosevelt wanted to fix the country, which was in bad shape. Unemployment had reached 25 percent, and, although it had dropped, it was still very high; thousands of banks had closed due to lack of liquidity; agricultural prices had fallen below the cost of production. Roosevelt and his administration took the first big steps toward what the Friedmans termed "government's role to serve as a parent charged with the duty of coercing some to aid others."

Regardless of his intentions, Franklin Delano Roosevelt violated the Constitution he had sworn to uphold. The perils of the time, he seemed to have reasoned, justified drastic measures that contradicted the wisdom of this nation's founders. Decisions and duties that had been intended to be the responsibilities of communities and local governments were taken over by a rapidly growing central government.

To the majority of Americans, it seemed that Mr. Roosevelt and his New Deal were a godsend. The economy was turning around. Gradually, Americans were feeling good about themselves and their country again. Roosevelt was elected to four terms as president! But not everyone saw the picture through the same lens. According to former President Hoover:

> Every collectivist revolution rides on a Trojan horse of "Emergency." It was a tactic of Lenin, Hitler, and Mussolini. In the collectivist sweep over a dozen minor countries of Europe, it was the cry of the men striving to get on horseback. And "Emergency" became the justification of the subsequent steps. This technique of creating emergency is the greatest achievement that demagoguery attains. The invasion of New Deal Collectivism was introduced by this same Trojan Horse.

Did Roosevelt's New Deal jobs programs really save the country? Here's the answer to that question according to Thomas J. DiLorenzo, associate professor of economics at

George Mason University and an adjunct scholar at the Cato Institute:

> The notion of government jobs programs first became popular in 1933 when Franklin D. Roosevelt decided to raise taxes and pay the unemployed for their attendance at government-run public works projects. There is a popular misconception that Roosevelt, by doing this, "put people back to work." The evidence, however, indicates that Roosevelt merely substituted government jobs for private sector jobs, as is always necessarily the case with government jobs programs. This made him very popular with the people who were given government jobs, but failed to alter the total level of unemployment during the Great Depression of the 1930s.

Besides the tragedy of the denigration of the Constitution in Roosevelt's mistaken effort to right the nation's economy, the other great calamity of that episode in our nation's history is that drastic measures that were officially taken to solve a temporary national emergency have become a permanent part of our everyday life ever since. And they paved the way for more of the same kind of runaway government growth. Once the floodgate had been opened, and then went unchallenged by "we the people," who truly make up the authority of the government, then the floods of government would swell until they would sweep away any challenges to the government's expansions.

With the mechanics of the process in place and the mindset of the majority in tune with the move toward a growing government, there seemed to be no turning back. No administration seemed able to resist the temptation to "do more" for Americans by instituting more government "helps." Few congresses seemed willing to stop the growth process—not to mention to turn things around and to move back to a Constitutionally restricted federal government. There was Lyndon Johnson's Great Society, with the subsequent creation of a new-housing bill, Medicare program, and the new federal Department of Housing and Urban Development. President Johnson increased America's involvement in another undeclared war. His predecessor, John F. Kennedy, had, without congressional authorization, sent seventeen thousand American troops into the Vietnam "conflict." By the end of his term, Johnson had increased that number to more than half a million American troops, also without congressional authorization.

Johnson, like Roosevelt, was fond of federal jobs programs. Again, these were well intentioned but misinformed attempts to cure the unemployment problem. But here is what Professor DiLorenzo has to say about government-created jobs:

> Public service employment is often characterized as "make work," pointing up the fact that people holding down such jobs often spend their time doing things for which there is really no demand or need. . . . Consider the following examples: . . .
>
> In Arizona, CETA [Comprehensive Employment and Training Act] paid college students to train for a track meet; in Bath County, Virginia, CETA workers were paid to attend dance classes; in Chicago, one CETA worker reported she was paid to "play checkers" with other employees; in Montgomery County, Maryland, a suburb of Washington, DC, and the wealthiest county in the nation, CETA paid nine women $145 per week to attend ballet school. . . .

Another sad fact is that these government jobs often do not go to the most worthy or needy but to those who have most loyally supported the elected government.

During the '80s, President Ronald Reagan had some success in tying up the monster. Although our current president has said that President Reagan's administration had "the worst job creation rate since the Great Depression," look at the statistics below for the revealing facts:

JOB CREATION BY ADMINISTRATION AND INCOME LEVEL
(1984 DOLLARS)

Percentage of jobs created paying:			
	Under $7, 012	$7,012 to $28,048	Over $28,048
Carter (1977–1980)	41.77%	68.2%	-9.9%
Reagan (1980–1984)	6.0%	46.2%	46.1%

Source: Joint Economic Committee, based on data from Bureau of Labor Statistics, US Department of Labor.

INFLATION

Fiscal Year	Annual Change in Consumer Price Index
1980 (The year before Reagan took office)	13.5%
1984	4.3%
1988 (Reagan's last year in office)	4.1%

Source: *Economic Report of the President* (January 1993), Table 13-59, p. 462.

It certainly appears that President Reagan had at least begun a process of corralling the economic monster. But the dangerous truth is, the monster is loose again, and now almost no one seems to be making a serious effort to corral it and put it back into the cage. The monster is still growing. It endangers our future—and that of our children.

Perhaps a time has come, as we will discuss in detail in later chapters, for Americans of all walks of life to rise up and reclaim their constitutionally given rights and authority. Americans need to raise their voices in dissent to runaway growth and lack of government's responsiveness to real American needs. We need to realize the truth in the words of former Senator J. William Fullbright: "In a democracy, dissent is an act of faith. Like medicine, the test of its value is not in its taste, but its effects." We need to reestablish our allegiance to the flag, which we used to repeat daily in America's classrooms: ". . . one nation under God, indivisible, with liberty and justice for all." May our united dissent to the current runaway government, one day restore this pledge in our nation's governmental system.

CHAPTER 8

THE DISASSEMBLY OF CURRENT MEDIA PHILOSOPHIES

> Whether a journalist is reporting a war or a grocery store holdup, it is not his business to consider whether the story will do good or harm. He has to have faith that, in the long run, the truth will do good.
>
> —*Andy Rooney*

At what point does the media cross the line from truthfully and accurately presenting the defining events of our lives, to arrogantly and cavalierly setting (unhealthy) trends for the masses to follow? Is the media becoming profit-driven at the expense of fairness and impartiality? Are some media outlets in danger of crossing the line from news delivery to propaganda dissemination?

The first Amendment to our US Constitution states: "Congress shall make no law respecting an establishment of religion, or prohibiting the free exercise thereof; or abridging the *freedom of* speech, or of *the press*; or the right of the people peacefully to assemble, and to petition the Government for redress of grievances" (emphasis added).

Our Historic Free Press

Our founders wisely saw the value of a free press. In a free society, people have not just a *right* to know about what's happening in their world—they *must* know. We cannot have a government "of the people, by the people, and for the people" if the people are uninformed. A free and unfettered press is necessary for the proper functioning of our republican form of government.

Certainly, few Americans would want the kind of society in which a few elite are so in control of that society and its media that they can spread lies to a largely duped public and go unchallenged by a free press. America has carefully guarded its free press. Most of us would abhor the very thought that our nation's media could ever become a propaganda machine like that which brainwashed Germany's citizens during World War II Nazism.

Under Nazism, the media's responsibility, as governmentally defined, was not to carefully investigate events and people and present the truth to an open and informed public. The Nazi media was a propaganda machine with the sole purpose of promoting the philosophy, teachings, and lifestyle of Nazism. Truth, under Nazism, was whatever Adolf Hitler and Joseph Goebbels—Hitler's information minister—said it was.

Under Nazism, without concern about challenge from a free German press, Goebbels could write, "The historic responsibility of world Jewry for the outbreak and widening of this war has been proven so clearly that it does not need to be talked about any further."[19] By the way, any time you read a statement from someone boldly proclaiming that his point is so well-proven that he need not document it, you can assume one of three things:

1. There is no proof for his assertion.
2. He is trying to coerce the reader into such a belief, so as to hide some truth.
3. He was too lazy to dig up the proof.

Nazism subtly turned the German press away from its duty to report factual stories that inform a free people, and into a machine that molded a new generation into indoctrinated soldiers who would serve the Furher and the Reich.

America's Vulnerability

Could such a thing happen in America? Probably not in the same way and to the same degree as it did in Nazi Germany. But our free press and the right of the people to know must never be taken for granted. If we blithely assume that our press unfailingly functions as an unbiased deliverer of all the news we need to be a free and informed people, our ignorance about this could be our undoing.

In an autocratic government, the biggest danger to a free press is almost always a lack of competition—the government severely restricts, or even controls, the few media outlets. Ironically, in America, the biggest danger regarding local TV news now is too much competition. Here's what Greg Byron, a former radio and television reporter, assignment editor, and producer, wrote about local TV news broadcasting:

> Before cable TV, the three network affiliates in each city had a virtual monopoly on viewers. . . .
> By around 1980, stations began hiring consultants to analyze ratings, conduct focus group surveys, and help

stations keep their viewers. . . . These consultants were not paid to recommend serious journalism. They were paid to get viewers. . . .

They told news directors that viewers were loyal to anchors [who] are familiar, friendly, attractive. . . .

While a student of Edward R. Murrow might want to lead a newscast with the most "important" story, the consultants urge local stations [to] lead their newscasts with the most sensational to grab viewers before they might be inclined to change the channel. Hence comes the phrase "if it bleeds, it leads."

In addition, according to Byron, "stations don't bite the hand that feeds them." Most local TV stations, out of fear of lost revenue, either ignore or gloss over any stories that might irritate any large advertisers. Byron also stated that most local TV stations are hesitant to air stories that might offend police, firefighters, or sports teams, because in so doing, they may see lucrative sources of easy information for other stories dry up in retaliation.

Although the competition at the national level is not quite as fierce, the situation there is not picture perfect either. Here, according to *Media Monitor*, are some pertinent facts and trends about network news during the nineties (1990–1996):

The top four topics of the nineties:

1. Crime: 9,391 stories on the network evening news shows
2. Economics: 6,673 stories
3. Health and medicine: 6,047 stories
4. The Soviet Union and Russia: 4,962 stories

Actually, the selection of topics and their coverage seems reasonable. But, as Greg Byron found with local news, *Media Monitor* also found at the national level: "If it bleeds, it leads." *Media Monitor's* report states: "The rapid rise in television's attention to crime is all the more striking when compared to actual crime rates during the same period. According to the FBI Uniform Crime Reports, the rate for serious violent crimes dropped 6 percent and the rate of crimes against property fell 10 percent in the United States between 1990 and 1995. . . ." (while in 1993 alone, the news coverage of crime stories doubled).

Could there be another reason why—besides the greedy grab for bucks through sensational images—the media would so increase its coverage of crime, even as crime rates were dropping? Ponder that question as we look at two more media trends as reported by *Media Monitor*.

1. While the unemployment rate dropped from 7.5 percent in 1992 to 5.4 percent in 1996, the number of news stories about the economy on national television news broadcasts dropped from a high of 1,457 in 1993 to 597 in 1996.

2. The percentage of stories from outside the United States on national news broadcasts jumped from a fairly static rate of about 30–32 percent prior to the Gulf War, to more than 50 percent during that war, but has steadily declined ever since to about 20 percent in 1996.

Now look at another media trend. According to Robert W. McChesney, "The global media system is now dominated by a first tier of nine giant firms. The five largest are: Time

Warner (1997 sales: $24 billion), Disney ($22 billion), Bertelsmann ($15 billion), Viacom ($13 billion), and Rupert Murdoch's News Corporation ($11 billion). . . . Firms like Disney and Time Warner have almost tripled in size this decade."

Why would an institution, dominated by a handful of megacorporations, want to paint a bleaker-than-real picture of America's situation, while at the same time reduce its coverage of foreign news? Take a look at another quote from Robert W. McChesney: "The two largest media firms in the world, Time Warner and Disney, generated around 15 percent of their income outside of the United States in 1990. By 1997, that figure was in the 30 percent to 35 percent range. Both firms expect to do a majority of their business abroad at some time in the next decade."

Could it be . . . is it possible that the media powers-that-be (those global megacorporations that "expect to do a majority of their business abroad in the next decade") have an interest in painting a bleak picture of a crime-ridden, economically depressed America, while ignoring the woes of the many other countries that are rushing toward a global economy and a global government? Is it possible that a power-hungry government finds little to object to when the media paints such a bleak picture because an ailing country can be convinced that it needs more help from the federal—or even world—government to cure those ailments?

TABLOID TV: UNRESTRAINED SENSATIONALISM

Not long after "traditional" television news media began the move toward "leads that bleed," a whole new genre of TV programming sprang up. These new programs, which purport to be "news magazines," have become better known as "tabloid TV." Like the more traditional media, tabloid

TV looks to grab viewers with graphic and shocking images. But tabloid TV has moved beyond traditional TV news. Tabloid TV also favors crime stories ("If it bleeds, it leads"). In fact, according to *Media Monitor*, one out of every four stories (25 percent) on tabloid TV programs (such as *Inside Edition, Hard Copy, Extra, and American Journal*), deals with crime. If tabloid TV buys into the "If it bleeds, it leads" theory, it quickly follows with, "If there's skin, it's in." According to the same *Media Monitor* report, sex-related stories on these programs run a close second to crime stories, with one in five stories (20 percent) featuring sex. In fact, many of the stories combine elements of crime and sex.

According to *Media Monitor*, of the many sex stories on tabloid TV, one-third were about extramarital affairs—particularly among the rich and famous. Is it any wonder that so many people defended President Clinton during his troubles with a White House intern by protesting, "Why pick on him; everybody does it?"

At the opposite end of the spectrum on tabloid TV, there are some "uplifting" stories, which make up a paltry 7 percent of the broadcasts. How many American families sit around after dinner in their family rooms digesting tabloid TV trash while they digest their meat loaf and mashed potatoes? Imagine how much better off this country could be if families spent tabloid TV time doing homework from school, discussing positive and virtuous character traits, reading uplifting books, or praying together. Does the phrase "a family that prays together stays together" bring new meaning in our society today?

PRINT ISN'T PERFECT EITHER

Newspapers are probably seen as the last holdout for conservative news-gathering methods and styles (if not in ideology). Simply by virtue of the delivery method, newspapers (and news magazines) cannot compete for immediacy with the electronic media. Consequently, print journalism concentrates, instead, on presenting issues in more depth (or at least sometimes tries to).

Newspapers are supposed to strive for clear, accurate, understandable, and unbiased presentation of what's happening around us. But in an increasingly busy and complicated world, editors have to make choices about what to fit into a limited number of pages. Simply by virtue of the necessity to pick and choose what to print and what not to print, editors are, unavoidably, censors.

Walter Lippmann, considered by many to be the dean of American political journalists, stated in an address to the International Press Institute, "Responsible journalism is journalism responsible in the last analysis to the editor's own conviction of what, whether interesting or only important, is in the public interest."[20] In other words, the editor of each newspaper decides for the public what is worth reading, based on who buys his newspapers. As I stated above, it's unavoidable; editors have to be censors who decide what belongs in front of your eyes when you pick up your newspaper—that is, those who do pick up and read a newspaper.

DECLINING READERSHIP

As recently as the midseventies, three out of four adult Americans read a newspaper every day. Now, less than a quarter-century later, fewer than half of America's adults read newspapers on a regular basis. There are undoubtedly many reasons for the decline, from increasingly busy schedules, to drops in literacy, to skepticism. Actually, skepticism about newspapers is not a new phenomenon; it's just more pervasive now. But look at what a few skeptics have said about their lack of confidence in newspapers:

> Never believe in mirrors or newspapers.
>
> —*Tom Stoppard*
> THE HOTEL AMSTERDAM, *1968*

> Once a newspaper touches a story, the facts are lost forever, even to the protagonists.
>
> —*Norman Mailer*
> ESQUIRE, *June 1960*

> All successful newspapers are ceaselessly querulous and bellicose. They never defend anyone or anything if they can help it; if the job is forced upon them, they tackle it by denouncing someone or something else.
>
> —*H. L. Mencken*
> PREJUDICES, *1922*

If you consider the names and backgrounds of those who made the statements above, you might dismiss them as literary elitists who disdain newspaper journalists as the blue-collar workers of writing. But print journalism has had its share of low points. In 1981, the *Washington Post* won a Pulitzer Prize for a tear-jerker story a reporter had written about an eight-year-old drug addict. The problem was the boy didn't exist. The *Post* returned the Pulitzer Prize, and the reporter resigned in disgrace. More recently, a *Boston Globe* columnist reluctantly resigned after his fabrications and plagiarisms were discovered. While most newspaper reporters have never, nor would they ever, deliberately lie to their readers, the pressure for recognition and promotions—not to mention less work through fabricating, rather than researching—will always be a temptation to all journalists and will always cause that bit of skepticism to linger with readers.

Beyond News

As we saw earlier in this chapter, many of the megacorporations that produce our news also produce our entertainment. For instance, Time Warner produces several news magazines including *Time*, but it also publishes books (including fiction), and it owns cable TV companies. Disney, known for entertainment, also owns the American Broadcasting Company and ABC News. Is this a healthy mix? Is it appropriate that the same corporations that bring us news also bring us books, music, videos, and movies that are increasingly loaded with unhealthy sex and violence? I don't think so.

But while we, the public, can't do much about such huge mixed-media conglomerates, we can do some things to help bring about a turnaround in the entertainment media and in the news media.

MAKE A STATEMENT WITH YOUR MONEY

Filmmakers believe "The 'G' rating is the kiss of death." In other words, movies that don't have some sex, violence, and/or profanity in them, will lose money because of low attendance. According to Dick Rolfe of the Dove Foundation, many moviemakers believe that they need to add at least a few profanities to G-rated movies to get them a PG-13 rating and increase attendance. Rolfe also quoted a top executive at a major film studio as saying, "Everyone knows that moms and dads won't accompany their little ones to a movie unless there's enough sex or violence or foul language for the grownups to enjoy."

Why would filmmakers believe such things about the viewing public? Simple. They're following the money. Does that mean that the Americans really do want entertainment that's full of sex and violence? Here's what Rolfe believes about this situation:

> Moviegoers have been compromising their standards for many reasons. First, parents are giving into the pressures of their little ones who carry on until they are allowed to watch the hip movie their friends are seeing. That brings us to the next reason. There is strong peer pressure among kids to be "cool" and see certain movies that are hyped to their age group by these studio marketers. And many well-meaning adults tell me that they put up with lots of swearing and immoral portrayals in PG-13 movies because there is such a dearth of high quality G and PG movies to enjoy. But, frankly, they wish they didn't have to be subjected to such gratuitous nonsense.

I have no idea what parents Mr. Rolfe talked to, but I see an even bigger problem in those families than selecting movies to watch. I have to ask, "Who's in charge of those families in which kids, prompted by slick promoters, choose the family's entertainment?" Sometimes, as parents, we need to "just say no." We need to come to the realization that parents can feed this vicious cycle by giving in to pleading children, who have almost no resistance to Madison Avenue manipulators trained to hook children with exciting promotions.

Here's how it happens: Hollywood releases two films at the same time. One is good, clean, wholesome, G-rated family entertainment that is advertised as such. The other film, rated PG-13, has an "attitude." It may not be overtly violent or sex-filled, but it has more than a couple of four-letter words, some playful violence, a lot of skin (with strategic parts barely covered), and lots of sexual innuendo. The ads focus on the "attitude" and make it appear to be really "cool." The kids are fascinated—as the promoters intended.

Some parents take their children to the movie (or allow them to go on their own). The kids who saw the PG-13 movie are viewed as being "cool" by those who haven't seen it. The "have-nots," feeling pressure to be as "cool" as the "haves," put pressure on their parents, many of whom give in. Ticket sales for the PG-13 movie skyrocket, while the G movie languishes. Message to filmmakers: attitude sells; wholesome bombs; make more PG-13 films; avoid G films.

You can write letters to the editor, to your congressional representative, or even to the movie producers. Those letters might do some good. But you can make the biggest difference in the types of movies Hollywood produces simply by being selective about your viewing choices. Hollywood duplicates what sells and avoids what doesn't.

"KURAULTING" THE NEWS BACK INTO LINE

The late Charles Kurault is almost revered by news people as well as the public. He was a marvelous storyteller whose simple eloquence held his viewers, listeners, or readers spellbound. And he knew a great story when he saw one (stories that lesser journalists often overlooked). Gary Gilson, executive director of the Minnesota News Council, remembered the following story about Mr. Kurault:

> After Dr. [Martin Luther] King [Jr.] was murdered, a white woman in Reno, Nevada, looked around and saw too many kids of color unoccupied and with no place to play. She had an idea—to build a park. But plenty of

people have good ideas and never make them real. She had an even better idea—a way to get it done. She said to her neighbors, "Let's build a park together, and let's do it in forty-eight hours."

Charles Kurault heard about it and did one of his CBS News "On the Road" pieces. That was more than twenty-five years ago, but I still remember the woman's name—Pat. She got merchants to donate building materials, and she motivated people from all over town to do the work. Kurault showed Pat trooping all over the field, encouraging people, including some teenagers enlisting an old Black man to hold one end of a plank that he was too feeble to carry himself.

At the end of the two days we saw a landscaped ballfield, a paved basketball court, and happy people using them. Kurault asked the old Black man what he thought of all that.

"The greatest thing about this isn't the park," he said. "It was building the park."

Gilson also wrote of Kurault, "Nowadays most of TV news sacrifices grace for pace. They think the opposite of sensational is boring. Kurault wasn't sensational, and he wasn't boring. Every time he thought, wrote, or spoke, he proved the value of context, precision, and fairness."

What more could Americans want from the media than context, precision, and fairness? What are we willing to promote with our dollars, and to what will we entrust our most valuable resources—our children to?

Retaking
Our America

CHAPTER 9

REKINDLE
THE AMERICAN DREAM

The foundations of our national policy will be laid in
the pure and immutable principles of private morality.
—*George Washington*

We saw in chapter 1 of this book that shortly after the
end of the Revolutionary War, newly independent America
was hard pressed to pay its soldiers. The brave men who
had risked their lives for the cause of freedom found themselves facing the tyranny of near-abject poverty. They didn't
ask for a government handout; they simply wanted to be
paid for their work as soldiers, as America's defenders. The
soldiers of the Revolution were ready to march on the capitol and were nearing the stage of another revolt to get what
was owed them. But following the costly war, the young
country was not in good economic shape.

George Washington again stepped forward to deliver
his country from a potential crisis. On March 15, 1783,
the disgruntled soldiers' former commander entered the
Temple of Virtue, a wooden hall built by the men, where
many of the unhappy troops were gathered to complain
and strategize. The soldiers held the general in high es-
teem. He had earned their respect as a man of integrity, a

man who seemed to belong in a Temple of Virtue. So the hall became quiet as the men waited for General Washington to speak.

Washington reminded the men about his own service with them. He had served, as we earlier saw, without pay. He beseeched them to be patient. He advised them that Congress would do right and that he would be their advocate. He implored them, "Let me entreat you, gentlemen, on your part, not to take any measures which, viewed in the calm light of reason, will lessen the dignity and sully the glory you have hitherto maintained." The great general had, in the Temple of Virtue, appealed to the men's sense of virtue—to their moral character. Washington well understood that it was the moral virtue and character of the nation's citizens that had made, and would keep, America great.

And it worked. It worked because George Washington truly was a man of virtue, of integrity. The men knew him well enough to know they could trust him. His words and his deeds were harmonious. Thomas Jefferson later stated, "The moderation and virtue of a single character probably prevented this Revolution from being closed, as most others have been, by a subversion of that liberty it was intended to establish."

Freedom Requires Responsibility

Thanks to the moral authority that George Washington wielded by virtue of his personal integrity, he saved the young nation from a potential internal strife that might have undone the republic almost as soon as it began. As we saw through the early chapters of this book, throughout its history, America has faced many crises, and in each case, it was the hard work and self-sacrifice of the majority of individual Americans that carried the nation through.

We also saw that Americans have never been perfect. As a people, we have made our share of mistakes, but even then we have rebounded, thanks to the wise guidance provided by our founding fathers, the generally high moral character of most Americans, and the grace of God.

We saw that perhaps the darkest chapter in our nation's history was the insistence of some Americans that they needed to, and had a right to, enslave other people whose skin was a different color—and the toleration of such a practice by other Americans. But when enough Americans of high moral character and good conscience said, "No, this must stop," things began to change. Probably no one in that crucial time was simplistic enough to think that such a grave national wrong could be righted easily. It would take tremendous personal and national resolve—and again, self-sacrifice.

President Abraham Lincoln spoke these words in December 1862, one month before he signed the Emancipation Proclamation:

> Fellow citizens, we cannot escape history. We of this congress and this administration, will be remembered in spite of ourselves. No personal significance, or insignificance, can spare one or another of us. The fiery trial through which we pass, will light us down, in honor or dishonor, to the latest generation. . . .
>
> We—even we here—hold the power, and bear the responsibility. In giving freedom to the slave, we assure freedom to the free—honorable alike in what we give, and what we preserve. We shall nobly save, or meanly lose, the last best hope on earth. Other means may succeed; this could not fail. The way is plain, peaceful, gen-

erous, just—a way which, if followed, the world will forever applaud, and God must forever bless.

It took a gruesome Civil War that, as we saw in chapter 4, required incredible sacrifices, including the lives of more than 600,000 brave Americans, but "the last best hope on earth" was "nobly saved"; the Union was restored, and slavery was abolished. America was free to develop into a nation in which, as Booker T. Washington said, "Character is power." Think for a moment about that statement by one of America's true heroes.

Booker T. Washington, an African-American who was born five years before the start of the Civil War—a man of unassailable moral character himself—did not sound this mantra we hear so often today: *"Knowledge* is power." No, Booker T. Washington understood that true power, power for good, is not in what we know, but in who we are inside. Some of history's vilest villains were full of knowledge but totally lacking in moral character.

CHARACTER: BUILT OR LOST, ONE STEP AT A TIME

Most of us have heard this wise and pithy saying: "Sow a thought, reap an action; sow an action, reap a habit; sow a habit, reap a character; sow a character, reap a destiny." People don't suddenly do a "Jekyll and Hyde" and turn from decent and honorable moral citizens into lawless rogues. Nor does the character of a nation change overnight. Each of us as individuals, and all of us corporately as a nation, change gradually and by degrees. It's like the old story of the frog in the kettle. If you drop the jumpy amphibian directly into a pot of boiling water, he'll quickly do his best to hop out. But if you set him in a pot of cool water and heat it gradually, he'll comfortably lounge as the slowly heating water brings him to his blissful demise.

If I choose to make one small omission in my favor while figuring my income taxes this year, next year it will be a little easier to make the same omission—and maybe a slightly larger one, too. If I choose to think about that attractive new secretary down the hall at work, it's only one more small step to dwelling on that thought, then to flirting, and then to . . .

Before the infamous serial murderer Ted Bundy was executed for his grisly crimes, he confided to well-known radio show host, author, and psychologist, Dr. James Dobson, that his obsessive problem started with something that by today's standards, unfortunately, is considered normal. He started by glancing at so-called soft-pornography magazines, such as *Playboy*. When he began looking at these magazines, he undoubtedly had no idea he would eventually graduate to sexually assaulting and murdering women all over the United States.

This gradual, frog-in-the-kettle descent into self-destruction can occur in the same way for a community or an entire nation. It has happened right here in the United States. We didn't become, overnight, a nation that looks to its government for everything, from financial provision in our senior years, to educating our children, to now providing our moral direction. Nor did we become, overnight, a nation that not only tolerates, but also provides federal funds for, killing unborn babies; nor a nation that tolerates sexually taking advantage of women, saying it is not a serious crime (as in the Clinton presidential impeachment debate). But even at the national level, each expedient determination, each decision that has been based on

short-term ease without regard for the long-term reper-
cussions, made the next one that much easier.

We have gradually lost sight of our basis of individual
and corporate responsibility to fulfill immutable, high moral
principles. We have gradually lost our personal, corporate,
and national character.

A person of true moral character recognizes that freedom without personal responsibility is license, and a licen-
tious people will inevitably be returned to bondage. If we
are going to recover and maintain the freedoms that our
government has gradually been usurping from us, we must
become an army—not an army of guns and tanks, but an
army of people of integrity, manned by a commitment of
personal values, such as those upon which this nation was
founded.

SOLDIERS OF VIRTUE

> Nothing is more important for the public wealth than to
> form and train youth in wisdom and virtue. Only a vir-
> tuous people are capable of freedom.
>
> —*Benjamin Franklin*

If we as a nation are ever going to turn the corner and
get back on track, if we are ever going to regain our greatness, it will not be through government-sponsored social
programs. Our national greatness can only be regained and
maintained through personal virtue and integrity. The greatness of our nation cannot trickle down from national programs and agendas; it must be built up from personal
strength of character, one citizen at a time.

As an individual among 250 million Americans, I, as a
single citizen, may not be able to wield much influence on
national policies, but I can have some influence; and like it

or not, I do have tremendous influence on those around me—we all do. Every decision that you or I make, whether it seems monumental or insignificant at the time, touches others and affects their lives. It is within my power (and yours) to make decisions that benefit others or that harm others. Generally speaking, if I choose the easy path, it may bring me short-term ease and comfort, but usually it will be a long-term detriment to me and those around me. High moral character usually requires hard work and hard decisions.

Let me remind us again of those seven principles that I believe led to America's greatness. We might even consider them as a rallying pledge for today's "Soldiers of Virtue."

1. Perform hard work as a consistent lifestyle.
2. Develop a thrifty lifestyle, and value the resources of this land.
3. Develop a sober lifestyle.
4. Develop an emphasis on the equality of all people before God and with respect to one another.
5. Practice as a duty, acts of doing good works for society's less fortunate.
6. Emphasize religious pluralism—respect for all denominations of religious belief.
7. Make a commitment to maintain personal standards of morality.

Read the following words of a modern-day soldier of virtue, Oklahoma Congressman J. C. Watts, from his address to the Republican National Convention in 1996:

> You see, character does count. For too long we have gotten by in a society that says the only thing right is to get by and the only thing wrong is to get caught.

Character is doing what's right when nobody is looking. And I want to make a promise to you.

We will do our best to leave this country in better shape financially, environmentally, and, most of all, spiritually.

The American dream is about becoming the best you can be. It's not about your bank account, the kind of car you drive, or the brand of clothes you wear. It's about using your gifts and abilities to be all that God meant for you to be. . . .

The American dream is the promise that if you study hard, work hard, and dedicate yourself, you can be whatever you want to be. You can do it. You are America's greatest resource. And one more thing. If a poor black kid from Oklahoma can be here tonight, this great country will allow you to dream your dreams, too. God bless you all.

Personal Character: The Key to Recovery

The first step in recovering our personal and national integrity is not fixing the blame on others. As syndicated columnist, Russell Gough, states, "Nobody wins when Americans play the blame game." Here's some of what Gough wrote about the "blame game" in his November 16, 1997 column, as printed in the *Ventura County Star*:

> How refreshing it would be, for example, to hear at least one candidate stand up and boldly take responsibility for his or her community's, state's, or nation's problems—instead of blaming those problems on the "foolish policies" or "incompetencies" or "lack of integrity" of one's political opponents.
>
> I especially have in mind taking personal responsibility for the ethical and moral poverty currently plaguing our great land. And on this particular issue, we citizens who are downright fed up with the way

our politicians incessantly point fingers and blame others for our ethical poverty probably have as much soul-searching to do as those we vote into—or out of—office.

How true, Mr. Gough, that we bear at least as much responsibility as our elected officials, especially when you consider these figures from a November 5, 1996, ABC News poll: 50 percent of those polled said they did not believe that President Clinton was trustworthy, and just 39 percent believed he was trustworthy; yet he was elected because, as found in that same poll, 50 percent of the respondents also said they believed that having a president who "cares about them" is more important than having a president of high moral character.

But look at what our second president, John Adams, had to say about the moral character of our leaders: "The people have a right, an indisputable, unalienable, indefeasible, divine right to that most dreaded and envied kind of knowledge—I mean the character and conduct of their rulers."

The preeminent issue of our day is character—the character of our elected officials and the character of the citizens who elect them.

Happily, there are churches, communities, and entire cities and counties here in the United States that have recognized the importance of the character issue. Columbia County, right here in my home state of Oregon, is one of the many communities that have responded to the need for high moral character in its citizens by instituting the Character First program.

Character First provides the schools, churches, cities, and communities that subscribe to its program, a monthly character trait—such as generosity, patience, or attentiveness—and then provides suggestions for teaching and mentoring those positive traits. In Baton Rouge, Louisiana, where the program has had some of its greatest successes, program presenters include the city's mayor, church leaders from a wide variety of denominations, and the president emeritus of a service coalition called 100 Black Men. According to an article in *The Greater Baton Rouge Business Report*, at just one participating Baton Rouge company, HollyTex, the dollar amount of workers' compensation claims dropped from $476,000 the year before they began the program to $47,000 two years after they began the program.

A similar program called CHARACTER COUNTS! was started in 1993 by the Josephson Institute of Ethics. CHARACTER COUNTS! is built around what it called the Six Pillars of Character: trustworthiness, respect, responsibility, justice and fairness, caring and civic virtue, and citizenship. According to CHARACTER COUNTS! literature, "Effective character education does not dismiss the importance of self-esteem, but maintains that ethical values must be ranked above expedience and personal preference."

CHARACTER COUNTS! advocates mentoring, such as that provided by the Big Brothers and Big Sisters programs, to help build the right character traits in young people. According to CHARACTER COUNTS!, a 1995 study found that youths in these mentoring programs were 46 percent less likely to abuse drugs, 33 percent less likely to hit someone, and 50 percent less likely to skip school.

Does character count? "It is character that supports the promise of our future—far more than particular government programs or policies," says former Secretary of Education William Bennett. Or in the words of that famous nineteenth-century American newspaper editor, "Fame is a vapor, popularity an accident, riches take wing, and only character endures." I believe that Americans are crying out, not for leaders who are more popular, and not for leaders who are more rich. Today our youth and our nation are crying out for leaders who are willing to take the pledge of following the seven moral principles on which this nation was founded. Not just in lip service, but in the day-to-day lives of those who would say they are worthy to serve this nation in political leadership.

I believe that there are those who are being raised up today who have the moral character to be entrusted as America's leaders. Americans need to be willing to exercise the power and authority they were granted in the Constitution to call and to elect these citizens of character into the leadership of nationally elected offices. We need to call on them first to show the fruit of their character by pledging to live their lives and governing this great nation under a promise and commitment to live by the founding moral principles of this country.

If we the people will hold those who seek office in this land to these standards, we will begin to see the seed of restoration of a new day of hope in our great land. May God once again be able to bless our land—land of the free and home of the brave. Let us exhibit this bravery through our votes and choices, calling and electing America's next leadership.

CHAPTER 10

REBUILD AMERICAN GOVERNMENT AND POLITICS

The major problem we face in our politics today is politicians who believe that it is more important to win than to tell the truth—that it is more important to win than to stand for truth before the American people!
—*Alan Keyes*

Alan Keyes, author, radio talk-show host, former US ambassador to the United Nations, and Ph.D. in government from Harvard, made the above statement during his speech to the Iowa State Republican Party Convention on June 12, 1998. Sadly, Mr. Keyes, a highly principled man who was conspicuously ignored by the mainstream press during his 1996 presidential bid, was right. Mr. Keyes is an enigma to the press; he is an extremely intelligent and well-educated African-American—and he is conservative.

According to the views of most journalists, educated Black men aren't supposed to stand for traditional American values, such as personal responsibility, strong families, self-sufficiency, and limited government. Consequently, one of America's smartest, wisest, and most capable leaders is largely unknown to the majority of American voters.

Perhaps if more Americans in 1995 had heard about Mr. Keyes, who he is, and what he stands for, we wouldn't be mired in the moral muck that now grips our nation. But how can a principled man, who plays by the rules and who refuses to lie or cheat, compete with political "lifers" whose sole goal is to get into a high-paying and prestigious public office and stay there as long as possible? How can an honest man, whose associates also are people of high moral principles, compete with media-savvy manipulators who are willing to do whatever it takes, with virtually no limits, to get their candidates elected?

Government for Sale

Here are some quick facts about the 1996 presidential campaign taken from the PBS *Frontline* episode "Washington's Other Scandal":

- Bill Clinton's campaign contributions totaled $20,342,966, with the largest single contribution being $132,250 from the accounting firm of Ernst & Young.
- Bob Dole's campaign contributions totaled $19,818,676, with the largest single contribution being $57,600 from CSX Corporation, a shipping company.
- In stark contrast, Alan Keyes's campaign contributions totaled $853,922, with no contribution exceeding $2,000, and most contributions being small amounts from individuals.
- "While the amount you can give directly to a candidate is tightly restricted, the amount you can give to a candidate's party is not. . . . This loophole [called *soft money*] in the federal election law has made it

possible for the parties to raise huge amounts through contributions to state party committees and the 'non-federal' bank accounts of the Democratic and Republican National Committees."[21]

The latest (devious) trend in using campaign funds for political advertising is so-called issue ads. Here's how the *Frontline* program explained issue ads:

An issue ad is, by definition, supposed to discuss broad political issues rather than specific candidates. In the landmark 1976 decision, *Buckley v. Valeo*, the Supreme Court created two broad categories of political advertising: express advocacy and issue advocacy. Express advocacy, as the name suggests, is advertising that explicitly recommends the election or defeat of a candidate. According to the court's decision, express advocacy ads are subject to federal campaign regulations. That means organizations sponsoring express advocacy have to abide by federal laws restricting the size of individual donations, barring corporate and union contributions, and requiring public disclosure of their contributors. But in the case of issue advocacy, the Court ruled that ads intended to educate the public on broader issues are protected by the First Amendment guarantees of free speech and are outside the reach of federal election laws. This means that the sponsors of issue ads are not required to publicly disclose the sources of their funding—and there is no limit on the amount of money any individual, union or corporation can contribute to an issue ad campaign.[22]

Have you already begun to imagine how unscrupulous "political animals" have twisted and subverted the Supreme Court's rulings regarding issue ads? In fact, according to that same *Frontline* program, Clinton's campaign strategist,

Dick Morris, worked out a crafty plan that allowed the Clinton campaign to funnel huge sums through the Democratic National Committee to be used for issue ads. They did this in spite of the fact that they had accepted $62 million of taxpayer money, with the stipulation that by accepting that money they were agreeing not to raise any more campaign money after the nomination. And, lest the reader think I'm implying that the Republicans were above such shenanigans, I'm not. Both parties are guilty. Both parties have found ways to manipulate the letter of campaign-financing laws in order to circumvent and subvert the spirit and intent of those laws.

Here's a little bit of what Joseph Lieberman, Democratic Senator from Connecticut, had to say about the matter in an interview with Bill Moyers:

[I]n my opinion, the most scandalous behavior that occurred in the 1996 campaign was legal. There was some illegal behavior, and people should be punished for that illegal behavior as a way to deter it from happening again, but if we don't change the law, then an awful lot of the worst stuff that happened in 1996, will happen again. It still is happening because people will feel that they got away with it. . . .

So I expect that if we don't change the law, the 2000 presidential [election] is going to be the biggest auction in American history, and what's going to be on the block is our government.[23]

According to the watchdog group called Public Citizen, the total spending by all candidates for federal campaigns in 1996 totaled more than $2 billion, a 33 percent increase over the 1992 total. And the "soft money" contributions in 1996 for the two major parties was $263 million, a whopping 206 percent increase over 1992! Every year it seems to get worse.

Is it any wonder that, even back in 1995, a poll taken by the Americans Talk Issues Foundation in the summer of that year, found that the following percentage of Americans distrusted our federal government for the following reasons:[24]

- It wastes money—93 percent
- Politicians tell people "what will get them elected"— 88 percent
- Tax laws help corporations more than people— 81 percent
- Politicians "do whatever they want" once they're elected—79 percent

LOTS OF TALK, BUT WHERE'S THE ACTION?

Clearly, there is a growing (and to a great extent, well-deserved) cynicism about government among the general population. Obviously, there is a very real need for reform. Politicians love to talk about the need for reforms of government, in general, and of campaign financing, specifically. Here's a sampling of what some current and former politicians have said about campaign financing:

> I don't think mistakes are just made at the edges. The entire process, even when conducted strictly within the law, invites corruption. . . .
> —*Former New Jersey Senator Bill Bradley*
> LOS ANGELES TIMES, *February 1997*

> Elections are more often bought than won.
> —*Indiana Representative Lee Hamilton*
> WALL STREET JOURNAL, *February 19, 1997*

Money! It is money! Money! Money! Not ideas, nor principles, but money that reigns supreme in American politics.

—*West Virginia Senator Robert Byrd*
NEW YORK TIMES, *March 20, 1997*

But what happens when it comes to actually doing something about it? A few (such as Washington State's third congressional district representative, Linda Smith), have fought hard actually *to do* something about it but with little real support from their colleagues. No, as I said in the previous chapter, change for the better in America will not first be instituted at the top and trickle down. In this nation *of the people*, good things usually work their way *up* from the grassroots level.

That's why we looked at the need for personal, individual moral character and integrity in the previous chapter before examining in this chapter the need for governmental changes. As *we the people* are ourselves committed to ethics and integrity, then we can demand and institute the same in our *government of the people*.

CHANGE AGENTS

Many of your friends and your neighbors (your fellow Americans) are already working to effect these changes from the grassroots level. Groups like Public Citizen and Silent Majority have organized to bring a new direction to our nation's leadership.

Public Citizen has long been committed to bringing about meaningful campaign finance reform, with the best solution being the public financing of federal elections. However, since public financing has little chance of passing under the current Congress, we will play a leading role in pushing for the best options for real reform this year—the McCain-Feingold bill (S.25) in the Senate and the companion Shays-Meehan (H.R. 3526) bill in the House of Representatives. These comprehensive bipartisan bills include a ban on so-called "soft money"—the unlimited, unreported contributions of special interests and wealthy individuals to political parties—provision to end the use of sham "issue ads" to evade limitations on campaign ads, and enhanced disclosure and enforcement.[25]

I will confidently state that these bills for campaign-finance reform that are, as of this writing, before Congress, would not be there but for the pressure of grassroots citizens' groups agitating for such reform. We the people can make a difference!

The silent majority need not—must not—be silent any longer. Just as the pressure of grassroots groups has prompted some in Congress to begin to give some serious consideration to campaign-finance reform, so our thoughtful, properly presented demands for general governmental reform can influence politicians to make positive changes. But we have to be involved. We can't go on allowing a vocal, and often radical, minority to dictate the policies that determine the direction of America. We must become aware and educated about the important issues that affect our country. We can't continue to be silent. In fact, if you're tired of being part of the silent majority, why not join the Silent Majority, Public Citizen, or some other grassroots political organization? According to Silent Majority's Web page:

> We felt that the truth was not really being told about political and current events. . . .

The purpose of the Silent Majority is to provoke discussion and thought about some of the current issues of the day, with a focus on politics. We at the Silent Majority do not claim to be unbiased, we have opinions and will let them be known. . . .

We are a non-profit organization and we receive no compensation for our work.[26]

Silent Majority's Web page has direct links to the following Web pages:

- Republican and Democratic National Committees, as well as the Libertarian Party
- The White House, the Senate, and the House of Representatives
- Embassies of the world
- The FBI, the CIA, Drug Enforcement Agency, and US Federal Government agencies
- Many others

Another group, called Citizens Against Government Waste (CAGW), takes on issues, such as, Medicare fraud, Patent Office "boondoggles," and Goals 2000 (a topic dealt with in chapter 5 of this book).[27] CAGW also has a Pledge of Integrity for candidates to sign.

At the local level, one of the best ways to get involved (without running for office) is by joining a Citizen Participation Group (CPO). According to the Washington County, Oregon CPO, a Citizen Participation Organization is "a place where you can discuss issues in a comfortable forum; meet neighbors who are interested in the community; get unbiased information; and find neighbors who will listen to your concerns and work with you to find solutions." The Washington County CPO meets monthly and discusses election issues, has candidate forums, gets updates from the local sheriff, and discusses land-use proposals.

But if all these grassroots public involvement groups are important for the renewal and maintenance of a free and honorable America, the easiest, most effective and available method for influencing the direction of this nation is, sadly, largely ignored.

Vote

> The death of a democracy is not likely to be an assassination by ambush. It will be a slow extinction from apathy, indifference and undernourishment.
> —*Robert Maynard Hutchins*

According to an August 12, 1998, Reuters News Service story, a group of Chinese who were invited by the Carter Center in Atlanta to observe an American election, got something less than they had bargained for. Only about 10 percent of the state's (Georgia) eligible voters turned out to vote in the election they were observing. The Chinese were stunned. They claimed that in their country, 90 percent of the people vote.

Despite the fact that the vote those Chinese observed was a primary with no real "glamour" races or initiatives, and despite the fact that free elections in many countries, such as China, are still relatively novel and (to these voting newcomers) exciting, the sad truth remains that Americans are woefully apathetic about voting. Only 49 percent of America's eligible voters cast a ballot in the 1996 election that determined our current president.

A study by the Medill School of Journalism on why Americans don't vote (particularly based on the 1996 elections) found that "they do not grasp the importance of elections on issues that matter to them, that they are ill-informed about their choices, and that they perceive the actual process of voting as difficult and cumbersome."

Perhaps, with the painful, and obviously dismal, moral climate we have recently seen in our nation's capitol, more among us will now begin to grasp the importance of elections. Perhaps, if more people who understand the clear connection between personal integrity and the national moral character take the time to vote and to encourage like-minded people to vote, we can begin to turn the moral tide in Washington, DC.

Although the Medill School study found a lack of understanding about the importance of elections on issues to be the primary reason for voter apathy among those who do understand that connection, a common reason for not voting was related to something we looked at earlier: abuses of campaign financing. Many potential voters have been turned off by what they perceive to be elections corrupted by money (and to a large degree, it is a correct perception).

But, regardless of the reason for not voting, failure to vote cannot eliminate the problems that discourage non-voters. Voting and involvement in grassroots political organizations may not solve the problems of election abuses. But failure to vote will not solve those election-abuse problems. If you have not been exercising your right and responsibility to vote, please think back over what you have read in the early chapters of this book. Think about the sacrifices our ancestors made to buy this right for you. Please don't squander your right to participate in this government of the people. Be the people!

One important organization that has formed to encourage more citizen involvement in the election process in general, and in voting specifically is called, simply, UVOTE.[28]

UVOTE proudly proclaims, "America's economic and social prosperity rest on the fundamental principles of our Declaration of Independence:

- God-given right of all Americans to life, liberty and the pursuit of happiness
- Our government exists to promote these rights
- Our government derives its power from the people's consent
- When our government or any other social institution fails to promote an abundant life for American citizens, we have the right to alter or abolish that institution"

UVOTE goes on to state, "Restoration of democratic control requires a more involved electorate, a more informed electorate, and a more empowered electorate." I encourage you to find out more about, and get involved with, groups such as UVOTE; many are listed in this chapter's endnotes.

If you become part of a grassroots political organization (or start one of your own), you might want to check out CapitolWiz.[29] According to CapitolWiz's Web page cover, it can provide your grassroots group "more than 2,500 pages of legislative and government information."

A similar helpful site for grassroots citizen groups to gain information is Votenet.[30] Votenet's Web page cover states, "New liberty is being won online with widespread technology and freedom of communication—one person at a time." Votenet's site includes a Legislative Action Center with the Congressional Directory; contact information for the fifty states' legislatures; congressional e-mail addresses; a search engine to find your congressman, using your zip code; and a congressional schedule.

The bottom line is this: while the American political process has grown a lot of warts, they won't go away if we ignore them. We must be involved for the good of our nation. And while the issues sometimes may be complex, our new technologies, such as the Internet, have made the facts more easily accessible for us to be more informed voters than we ever have been before.

Despite all the newly available and easily accessible grassroots groups, an article in the October 11, 1998, issue of *The Sunday Oregonian*, written by Michael J. Gerson, says, ". . . probably fewer than 5 million Americans [he calls it a mini-electorate] will decide the November election."

How abhorrent it should be to Americans that such a small fraction of "we the people" will determine who will be the elected officials making crucial decisions and laws as we enter such a crucial time for our nation. Do you realize that with these kinds of voter turnouts, it would take only a fraction of America's silent majority to elect people who hold the high moral values and principles that are so important for America's survival?

A New American Declaration of Independence

In chapter 12, we will explore the Eight Principles of a New American Declaration of Independence in greater detail, but here is a summary of them now for your consideration:

1. Apolitical/nonparty-aligned election of federal government
2. Restore grassroots citizen control to American government
3. Establish a "care umbrella" for all tax-paying Americans

4. Reestablish the concepts of our national heritage and history to American education
5. Establish national policies to obtain and maintain a nation free of national debt
6. Promote the Seven Basic Moral Principles upon which America was founded
7. Reestablish a united nation working for the benefit of all its citizens
8. Regive the gift of American independence to the next millennia of Americans

As I will elaborate on in chapter 12, it is imperative that each of us be willing to move from the ranks of the silent majority and to be Americans willing to use our right and duty to vote to make a change. This Agenda of Eight, as I call it, needs to become a rallying point for Americans to hold high as a standard for reclaiming America. Together, we can lift the standard so high and so loud that this agenda will become the battle cry for Americans everywhere, making a new declaration of moral independence for Americans in all walks of life, standing proudly, as together, we enter the new millennia.

ENOUGH IS ENOUGH

Let me share with you a story I believe portrays why it is so important for every American to realize their part in becoming active in their local communities (as well as in the local and national political arena) to battle to restore the values that made America a great nation.

According to the story, Satan and his lackeys are planning to keep people from improving themselves and obtaining their God-given goals. After much debate and many suggestions, Satan stands. The cagey deceiver raises his hands to silence the crowd in the great hall. As a solemn hush falls, Satan bellows, "It's simple; we'll just encourage inventions and the productions of things that will cause people to be so engrossed that they will become entrapped in them. There will be televisions to engross and mesmerize. We will provide addicting computer games and the Internet. Our goal will be to entice people to get lost in trivial entertainment."

Another silence fell as the listeners digested their master's plan. "In other words," Satan continued, "we will lure people to get so involved in silly things that they will have no time for important events—or for one another."

The crowd roared and cheered as they anticipated their involvement in their master's insidiously clever scheme to divert people from ever doing anything of life-changing significance.

Sadly, we find people everywhere who complain about how their lives have become too busy to accomplish the things that they know deep down are really important. Have we indeed fallen into the devil's trap?

And while sincere, hard-working, but duped people have fallen into this trap, others have pushed a subversive agenda to the forefront. These people are working (sometimes subtly, sometimes almost brazenly) to force their well-planned agendas to control all Americans' lives. Even though most Americans would oppose such schemes in principle, the agendas move ahead because good men and women (believe they) are too busy to oppose them (or often are too busy even to be aware of them). Consequently, the solid moral principles upon which this country was founded are in danger of being lost in the frantic shuffle.

When will we awaken and notice that we are on a precarious precipice that is in danger of crumbling from under our feet? When will we replant our moral roots? We may not have much time left.

It's time to step back from the crag and take a stand. It's time, as a united people, to let this nation and our government know that we will no longer tolerate experiments with the future welfare, happiness, and freedoms of our children. Americans who value honor and freedom must stand up, get utterly angry, and through the powers granted in our Constitution say, "Enough is enough!"

For those who might say that I've gone too far, let me share an example from the Bible. People of other faiths, as well as Christians, regard Jesus Christ as perhaps the humblest and most pious of men. Yet the twenty first chapter of Matthew's gospel records the account of Jesus entering the temple, and with a righteous anger, driving out the merchants. He called them thieves and robbers as he cracked a quickly crafted whip after the fleeing traffickers.

Have we achieved that kind of anger the kind that will break Satan's spell of indifference in our lives? Will we break free of the entrapment of things that have taken control of our time and our priorities? Are we angry enough to retake control of our lives and America's future?

PRIORITIES

"A hundred years from now, it will not matter what my bank account was, the sort of house I lived in, or the kind of car I drove. But the world may be different because I was important in the life of a child" (Successories, Inc.).

Let us propose that the next generation of American children will see a different America! Let us also purpose that the process of this change will begin right now, right here, with you!

You see, I too have a vision. I see Americans of all backgrounds, races, and religions who are willing to see that vision too. It's a vision of an America restored to high standards by its people. Driven by moral principle, this nation will uphold the weak; it will desire justice above wealth; and above all, it will once again become one nation under God, indivisible, with liberty and justice for all. It's a vision of a nation where my grandchildren and yours will stand side by side, and as America's flag goes by, they will say, "My parents and grandparents made a difference." They will be able to say, "That is why I stand here free and with dignity today."

Some might ask, "Are we so far gone that we have lost hope that America can find its way back and preserve the freedoms and principles on which it was founded?" No, not if we act soon. Can the great experiment of freedom, self-government, and democracy be revived? Yes, when we, as Americans, will unite and work together.

In chapter 12, I will elaborate on some suggestions that we can participate in that I believe will provide a starting point for restoring the greatness of our America. Together *we can make a difference!*

CHAPTER 11

RELEASE FROM NATIONAL DEBT

I, however, place economy among the first and most important of republican virtues, and public debt as the greatest of the dangers to be feared.[31]
—Thomas Jefferson

At the time of this writing, 10:54:21 A.M. PDT, October 15, 1990, the outstanding public debt is $5,528,815,545,337.83. That's *five-and-a-half trillion*, plus change. That equates to $20,413.89 of debt for each of America's 270,835,963 citizens (men, women, and children). And the national debt has been increasing at a rate of $642.6 million per day since President Clinton took office in 1993! We are in grave danger.

Don't let the current "Pollyannaish" platitudes from our nation's capitol about a budget surplus fool you; things are not getting better. The fact is, the single biggest appropriation in the proposed 1999 budget is for the Treasury Department to get the money to pay *the interest* on the national debt. That's right, more money is allocated for the interest on the national debt than for Health and Human Services, the Department of Defense, or for the Agriculture

Department. The 1999 budget calls for *$400 billion just to pay the interest on the national debt—for one year!*

It is no wonder that Thomas Jefferson is also quoted as saying: "I wish it were possible to obtain a single amendment to our Constitution. I would be willing to depend on that alone for the reduction of the administration of our government to the genuine principles of its constitution; I mean an additional article, taking from the federal government the power of borrowing."[32]

How did we get into this mess? Here's a very easy-to-understand explanation by Gene Simmons, Founder of the National Debt Awareness Campaign: "Each year since 1969, Congress has spent more money than its income. The Treasury Department had to borrow money to meet Congress's appropriations. Now the total borrowed is about $5,500,000,000,000. That's five trillion dollars [plus]. It's called the national debt."[33]

The talk of a budget surplus that has most of the politicians and bureaucrats in Washington clamoring for their share of the credit is a cruel illusion—a con game. The truth is, that so-called surplus is money plundered from government trust funds—not the least of which is the Social Security trust fund. That's right, *our president wants to use money pillaged from our Social Security trust fund to rescue Social Security.* And in our increasingly busy and complex world, most Americans will blissfully believe the fantasy and go their merry way, thanking their lucky stars that our brave president has saved our future by saving Social Security.

But here's what Senator Ernest Hollings had to say about the matter, in a speech he gave in January of 1998:

> The thrust of President Clinton's State of the Union address was "save Social Security first." The quickest way

to save Social Security is to stop looting Social Security. Over the years, we have looted the Social Security trust fund with wild abandon; we owe it to the tune of $631 billion right this minute. It should be a $631 billion surplus. . . .[34]

Folks, if you have been counting on Social Security to provide for your old age (or even as a supplement for your old age), you will be sorely disappointed. In his book *The Best Kept Secret in America*, William A. Stanmeyer quoted the following from his accountant's newsletter: "Of every 100 people reaching age 65, one will be wealthy; nine will have income between $15,000 and $24,999; thirty-three will be dead; and fifty-seven will be '*dead broke*.'"

It doesn't have to be like this. Like the stubborn, but resourceful mule we saw in the introduction of this book, we can get out of our grave of national debt. How is this possible? How can we accomplish such a feat? *Only by working together in a united way so as to forge a union of Americans in all walks of life, that will enable us, once we have filled in the abyss, to establish a pattern to avoid redigging the debt again.* So what is the miracle formula? Why has no one in the history of our national debt ever proposed doing this before? What does this require of us as individuals? And how do we go about incorporating it before it is too late?

This solution must be one that Americans, while working together in unity, can help create. The first objective is to create a policy to provide freedom from this smothering debt. Second, we must elect a team of governmental leaders who are determined to carry out the will of the people to achieve a policy of converting our debt into a financial freedom for all Americans. Americans must be willing to go to the electoral polls and create, through their personal electoral powers, a leadership team that will work together with its fellow Americans to build a new America and have a second Declaration of Independence.

Our country needs a declaration that would initiate a revolution to reinstate the American goal for a government *of* the people, *by* the people, and *for* the people. Americans need to make their own individual declaration of a new American Independence Day. The year 2000 can be an American celebration of declaring independence from the mounds of national debt and from a governmental system that has lost touch with the American citizens it is supposed to represent.

Let me illustrate from an experience in my own life. I started my first business, a retail store, in the early '70s. I was as proud of that little store as a father with a newborn (a glorious event I would experience a few years later). I can remember taking people by my store just to show it off. I couldn't have been happier!

But soon the realities of being a small-business owner began to hit home. The installments on the money I had borrowed to start the store needed to be paid. The weekly, as well as monthly, routine payments became a regular grind. And yet, despite all of the mounting payments and management struggles, in about six to seven months, I began to see a small payback. Normally, a new business is very fortunate if it realizes a profit before the end of the first year; my little store was turning a profit in just slightly over half a year! My pride grew as I counted my first meager profits, oblivious to the fact that a few profits did not necessarily set a trend. Glowing in my newfound euphoria, I didn't realize that a major challenge would soon appear on the horizon. Like so many things in life, some of the major challenges can never be fully anticipated, as I was about to discover.

That summer, as I began my eighth month in business, I started on a process that would eventually lead to a strategy of debt retirement, a strategy I would share with many over the years. This was the summer of the 1970s oil embargo. Gas lines became the newest phenomenon, with some people actually spending the night in their cars to be assured of getting gas as the stations first opened in the morning. It was against this backdrop that my little business entered its eighth month in a small automotive manufacturing community in west Michigan.

Michigan is known for many things. One of them, at that time, was a major economic dependence on the automotive industry. Many of the employers in west Michigan relied almost completely upon the national automotive industry. Soon, as the oil embargo continued, a familiar trend began to reappear out of the normal annual cycle of industry slowdowns and layoffs: Many of the automotive manufacturers were starting to let their employees go. As they cut back on their work force, the smaller retail stores began to feel the impact. Before long, the rising unemployment was being reflected in the cash register sales of my own little store.

As my sales began to wane, I tried diversifying the type of products I sold. Unfortunately, at this early stage of the store's life, it did not have the working capital to make this change rapidly enough. Since I had already borrowed quite heavily to open the store, I found I could not borrow anymore to make this needed change. Day after day, I became painstakingly aware that I would have to make some major changes. I laid off one of my employees and began working even more hours myself. Soon I was working about eighty hours a week, but I still was not able to make enough sales to keep the store at a break-even point. Even as I continued to hope for a last-minute miracle, I slowly conceded that the only answer was to swallow my pride and make arrangements to close the store.

As I notified my vendors and employees, I could feel the anger and self-doubt rising within me. I was so sure God had directed me to start this business, and yet now I found myself packing up everything in the store to deliver to someone I had sold it to for pennies on the dollar. My dream was dead, and my heart was broken. This was a loss that, at times, still haunts me today. Mounds of bills and payments that were due, soon replaced all my savings, hard work, and dreams. The necessity of coping with these debts brought me face-to-face with a new reality. There were remaining utility bills, federal and state taxes, vendor bills, and the never-ending bank payments. It seemed as if in my unemployed state, I would soon drown in this sea of debt.

As I searched for and found work, with God's help I began to put together a plan for dealing with my financial obligations. I negotiated new payment arrangements with my creditors, many of whom were extremely cooperative. Others, primarily the state and federal governments, were a bit more difficult to deal with. Eventually, however, I was able to begin the process of chipping away at the mountain of debt that towered over me.

During this process, I learned some skills that would later have potentially bigger implications. One of the things I learned was that if I could reduce the interest on my debts and combine existing payments by means of a debt-consolidation loan, the repayment process would be accelerated. I sold my newer car and replaced it with an old clunker, so I could take my car payment and apply that money to a business debt. Each item I restructured to reduce my payments, soon helped generate an enthusiasm in paying off the entire debt. I soon began to feel as if I was using a bulldozer to lop off whole sections of this mountain of debt, which I felt I had started chipping away at with a spoon. Within about eighteen months, I felt as if the mountain had been reduced to a molehill, and I was beginning to feel a relief from the burden I had been carrying.

In addition to what I experienced as a small-business owner in the '70s, I have faced other business and financial challenges in my professional life, which I believe have prepared me to address the challenge we face as Americans today. Because of the government's seeming attempt to downplay the implications and ramifications of the enormity of our national debt, most Americans have yet to experience the personal impact of that debt, such as I did on a lesser scale as a small businessman. However, if this issue is not addressed, and a credible plan is not developed soon, each and every American will feel its weight and impact in the very near future.

To some extent, many Americans are already experiencing the fallout from this mountain of debt, which currently competes with potential homeowners, business owners, students seeking a higher education, and those simply trying to better their station in life. How? By competing for a limited supply of savings and investments available today. By taking trillions of dollars out of circulation for public and private use, this burgeoning national debt already affects each and every one of us, whether we are aware of it or not. This escalating problem causes mortgages and other types of loans to carry higher interest rates than they would without the competition of the national debt. Loan standards are higher, thereby reducing the number of those who can qualify to receive loans. There is a higher degree of uncertainty about what funds will be available to finance our health and retirement needs as hoped for through Medicare and Social Security. These and many other day-to-day problems are a direct impact of the overwhelming nature of the current national debt.

In addition to the national debt, which is, as I previously pointed out, currently in excess of 5.5 trillion dollars, there is an unfunded, yet implied, contractual liability associated with Medicare, Social Security, and the national public service retirement program for governmental employees, bringing the combined debt and liabilities of the national government in 1997 to about 14.5 trillion dollars. The daily interest on that amount is approximately $828,767,123. At a conservative interest rate of 5.5 percent, that equals about 302.5 billion dollars annually, a sizable chunk of change that is multiplying and eating away at every individual American's future. This constant drain of capitol severely limits the availability of money for necessary and productive investments, and it is eroding our national economy as well as the American Dream.

We are currently paying the interest on just the national debt as a line item in our national budget. Suppose we began to use these interest payments as a source of funds to start the repayment process. My suggestion would then be to give each American a monetary gift, in the form of some sort of trust fund, equal to the individual's pro-rata portion of the national debt. To see how this would work, let's calculate this amount and look at an imaginary American family with a combined income of $40,000. Using the payments on the interest of the national debt, these payments are used to pay on a small portion of the principal of the national debt. For every $40,000 of national debt principal paid off in this manner, the government would issue to tax-paying American citizens a $40,000 trust note, earning interest at a fixed amount, possibly 6.5 percent. This method would work because the trust note would replace actual notes owed by the government as part of the national debt. Further, this trust note would replace an implied liability for those people holding the trust notes in the old Social Security system.

This trust note eventually would be able to take the place of Social Security as a disability and retirement plan. In fact, tying this into other components of the plan, it eventually could replace our current Social Security and Medicare programs with a guaranteed source of income and even greater potential for actual retirement income. Additionally, it could fund a disability and hospitalization program that would be portable as people moved from job to job or location to location. I will explain my thoughts on the proposed specifics of these programs in the next chapter, after I present their practicality.

At the above rate, we would be able to establish a trust plan for 7,562,500 tax-paying Americans each year. The interest on the remaining national debt principal would be paid from funds saved and not needed to be paid into the old Social Security program. Since there would not be a liability associated with Social Security and Medicare for these 7,562,500 people each year, from that point in time, the employer's portion of taxes going into the Social Security fund for these 7,562,500 Americans could be used to pay the associated interest on the national debt. Assuming there are 180 million tax-paying Americans, it would take approximately twenty years to convert the national debt into a trust fund system.

14,500,000,000,000.00	Combined National Liabilities
5,500,000,000,000.00	National Debt Component
302,500,000,000.00	Annual Interest
25,208,333,333.33	Monthly Interest
828,767,123.29	Daily Interest
7,562,500.00	People per year obtaining a trust-note program
23.80	years to pay off current national debt. (Does not take into account a reduction of the debt and the interest necessary to repay it. This factor should reduce the time to less than twenty years.)

The first question this proposal raises for the elderly is, of course, what would happen to their current Social Security and Medicare payments? The simple answer would be, *nothing*. The taxes that could fund their portion of Social Security funds are still being paid into the fund, and the balance in the Social Security fund would remain there in sufficient amounts to guarantee their payments. The matching portion of employer's Social Security and Medicare payments for those not yet converted to the trust-note program would still be paid into the fund. Periodic, calculated adjustments would need to be made from time to time, but the current commitments could be maintained for this generation. There would, of course, need to be a cutoff point calculated as to exactly what age and when the plan would be implemented for people working today. Within about twenty years, through this trust note program, every working American would begin to have retirement and hospitalization needs cared for from the investment of these funds.

This means that Americans who are in their twenties today could have a better and more substantial disability, retirement, and hospitalization program than what is currently available, with many potential side benefits besides. Wouldn't that be a wonderful prospect? In fact, this program would even create benefits that exceed the income available through the current Social Security system for those in their forties, should they chose to retire when they reach their sixties—a dim prospect under the current system

There are several reasons such a program is not already in existence today. The primary reason is the power of the national bureaucracy to preserve itself at the expense of the everyday American tax-paying citizen. Another reason is the political fighting of special interest groups and elected officials, seeking to protect funding for their pet governmental pork-spending programs. An even greater reason is for politicians to minimize the panic that could be caused if Americans realized how much the current budgets are dependent on siphoning off Social Security monies to fund their pet spending projects. But are these reasons sufficient to deny ourselves, our children, or our children's children a brighter and more prosperous future, free of a national debt that threatens to crush them at any moment? I don't think so!

The greatest challenge to getting this program implemented is not a financial one. There are many benefits and national budgetary-cost savings that can be created to make the trust-note program more feasible if necessary. The real challenge is to create an electoral uprising by Americans that will get this plan fully approved, researched, and operating within the next four years. Currently, for every four years of delay, approximately another 1.25 trillion dollars will be added to the national debt.

Some might say that applying Neumann's proposal, which we looked at in the Introduction, to use the current national budget surpluses to reduce the national debt could accomplish the same things as the program I have proposed. I believe that using the budget surpluses in this manner could certainly be part of the process that would make a national trust-note program an even greater success. However, trying to reduce the national debt, using only the budget surpluses, would be like tossing a pebble into the world's oceans. We need more. We need unity. We need a corporate effort that would include all Americans. And we need it now.

Not long ago there was a popular box-office thriller titled *Independence Day*. This movie, an industry success story, captured the American imagination as it portrayed Americans uniting to achieve a common cause. However, a Declaration of Independence in the second millennia is not an independence from some unknown alien force or some undefined hidden enemy. It is an independence from a way of thought that has placed a stranglehold on the citizenry by way of a governmental "old thinking" bureaucracy. Americans need to become free of this "old thinking" and be willing to forge together an American unity. In doing this, we can achieve national goals, as well as the development of a structure and tools that will guarantee the future welfare of every tax-paying American. Together we can regain an America governed of the people, by the people, and for the people—and meeting the needs of Americans today.

But it must begin with each of us—right here, right now, right away. Are you willing to be a part of America's newest Declaration of Independence?

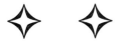

CHAPTER 12

FOR OUR CHILDREN:
REDECLARE
AMERICA'S INDEPENDENCE

Who kept the Belgians' black bread buttered?
Who fed the world when millions muttered?
Who knows the needs of every nation?
Who keeps the keys of conservation?
Who fills the bins when mines aren't earning?
Who keeps the home fires banked and burning?
Who'll never win a presidential position?
For he isn't a practical politician?
Hoover—that's all!

Well, that's not bad; the *Chicago Daily News* got seven out of eight right in the above-cited poem published in 1923. But the newspaper was wrong on one key point: Herbert Clark Hoover, one of the most admired people in the world for a time, *did* win a presidential position, and America was a better place for having elected him.

The Champion of Individual Responsibility and Volunteerism

The vilification many have visited on Hoover's memory is wholly unwarranted. As I stated earlier in this book,

Herbert Hoover had been president just half a year when the Great Depression hit. That worldwide economic disaster did not develop overnight.

Hoover was born into a devout Quaker family in Iowa. And although he was orphaned at age ten, his Quaker roots played a great part in directing the course of his life—as did his being orphaned. After growing up with Quaker relatives in Oregon, Hoover chose to enroll at Stanford University in California and study geology and mining.

At Stanford he met and married Lou Henry, who had pursued the same majors as Herbert. Together they managed mining operations in western Australia and China. They were millionaires before they reached their fortieth birthdays. Then when a Serbian peasant assassinated Austria's archduke, it was the beginning of World War I. The world would be changed forever, and so would Herbert Hoover's life.

One of Hoover's first actions after the outbreak of the war was to organize the return of thousands of stranded Americans to the United States. Hoover had an abiding faith in his fellow Americans to do the right thing in times of crisis, so he persuaded nine friends to join him in making loans, totaling $1.5 million, to pay for the return of those stranded Americans. His faith was proven to be better than 99 percent accurate, when all but four hundred dollars was repaid.

After rescuing his fellow Americans, Hoover then turned his attentions to the other victims of the war. First on this list were the citizens of neutral Belgium, caught between Germany and France. Hoover left behind his lucrative mining operations and devoted himself to war-relief efforts—and he did it with two stipulations: (1) he would receive no salary; and (2) he would be unobstructed in his organization and administration of the Commission for the Relief of Belgium.

Throughout the war, Hoover made forty trips to London and Berlin to persuade the belligerents to allow relief supplies through. But perhaps the most remarkable aspect of Hoover's relief work was that he depended more on Americans' voluntary cooperation than on coercive taxation—the entire government budget for the Food Administration was just eight million dollars. Hoover persuaded Americans to make personal sacrifices for the sake of the European Allies. Having himself been an orphan, Hoover was especially sensitive to the plight of children. It has been estimated that Hoover's war-relief work saved the lives of between fifteen and twenty million children.

By 1920, Hoover was so highly regarded that both major political parties wanted to nominate him. In fact, Franklin D. Roosevelt, a Democrat, said, "[Hoover] is certainly a wonder, and I wish we could make him President of the United States. There could not be a better one." But Hoover was a Republican, and astonishingly, the Republicans nominated and subsequently elected Warren G. Harding. Hoover became Harding's Commerce Secretary. And when, after two and a half years of mediocrity culminated by an administrative scandal, Harding suddenly died, he left "Silent Cal" Coolidge at the nation's helm. Hoover continued as Coolidge's Commerce Secretary.

One of Hoover's campaigns as Commerce Secretary that was somewhat derided at the time, but for which we can now be grateful, was the standardization of products. Standardization dramatically reduced production costs and increased productivity.

When, at the end of his first full term, Coolidge announced his decision not to run again for president, Herbert Hoover became the logical candidate for the Republican Party. Although some of his fellow Republicans encouraged

Hoover to make an issue of his opponent's Catholic faith (America had never elected a Catholic President), Hoover refused to do so, choosing instead to campaign on the issues and on his record of service. Even though he refused to sling "political mud" he was elected the 31ˢᵗ president of these United States.

Sadly, however, Hoover is now best known for being in office when the Great Depression struck. But in spite of the Depression, Hoover had many remarkable accomplishments.

Perhaps his greatest achievement as president—in spite of the Depression—was his reformation of banking laws, and especially the establishment of the Reconstruction Finance Corporation (RFC). The RFC was officially titled, "An Act to provide emergency financing facilities for financial institutions, to aid in financing agriculture, commerce, and industry, and for other purposes."

But the main thrust of Hoover's plans for recovery called not for massive government bailouts, but for changes and sacrifices in the private sector. In a speech he gave in August 1932, Hoover declared, "It is not the function of government to relieve individuals of their responsibilities to their neighbors, or to relieve private institutions of their responsibilities to the public, or of local government to the states, or of state governments to the Federal Government. . . ."

I am confident that if the American voters in 1932 had held on to their faith in Herbert Hoover, he would have led them to a complete economic recovery—and without the massive government bailouts that started America on the road to becoming a nation full of people who expect their government to provide for them. Folks, *we are the government*, and as Herbert Hoover said, "It is only by this release of initiative, this insistence upon *individual responsibility,* that there accrue the great sums of individual accomplishment which carry this nation forward." America can only be as good as the sum of its parts (each individual American).

America's Restoration Blueprint

After we have established the rock-solid foundation of personal moral character as a true basis upon which to build and choose leadership, we are ready to focus seriously on steps that can lead us in reclaiming an America *of the people, by the people, and for the people.* While we will not rebuild America through formulas, a well thought-out blueprint under the guidance of those who possess moral character based on the seven moral founding principles of this nation (as outlined earlier in this book) can guide our united efforts. Let me share with you a blueprint, which I call the "Agenda of Eight" that can provide a basis for America's restoration:

1. RESTORE GRASSROOTS, AMERICAN CITIZEN CONTROL OF THE POLICIES AND DIRECTION OF OUR GOVERNMENT

In previous chapters, we have looked at how, in this century, many in the American government have steadily promoted a biased agenda. They have sought to remove authority and control from the people by transferring it to government bureaucracy and special-interest groups.

They have disassembled the constitutional foundation of our government as expressing the intended will of *"we the people,"* to that of the expressed will of those who have the best political connections.

These special interests include lobbying groups who use political contributions, gifts, promises of work and funding after leaving office, and other enticements to exercise undue influence over elected leaders, who are supposed to represent all of the people who elected them. If this current system is to change, Americans must unite in going to the polls and supporting candidates who will restore honor and integrity to government. We must elect Americans of moral character who are willing to exercise the American founding principle of an elected citizenry serving their fellow Americans for a specified time in a political office, as opposed to electing those whose goal is to achieve full-time bureaucratic status.

Once we have regained citizens' control of this great government, I believe we need to do a "jobs justification" of each and every job in the federal government. We need to redefine the functions of all departments and jobs with this being the standard: "Does this department or job support the constitutional authority of the American people?" If the answer is no, then it should be redefined to do so, or it should be eliminated.

Another possibility, whose time may have come, is to exercise the constitutional authority to make amendments to the Constitution. Perhaps the time has come to consider exercising this option in encouraging the Congress to allow certain national issues to be duly brought through a process for being placed before the people as a national referendum. If *we the people* are the true authority of this government, then there ought to be times when the people's voice should be heard directly, as opposed to being interpreted for them by others. This could help restore Americans' confidence in the idea that they do count, that their voices can be heard, and that they can make a difference.

I firmly believe the numbers and the research show that the principles espoused in this book are achievable goals. What's lacking is the united electoral power of at least 5 million Americans (as noted in chapter 10), who will support the candidates who support these long-needed reforms of American government. If you have not already done so, please make a commitment to register to vote, and then use your vote to make your voice heard throughout America and around the world.

2. PROMOTE AN APOLITICAL PARTY UNITY IN AMERICA TO BRING UNIFIED ATTENTION TO THE BASIC PROBLEMS IDENTIFIED IN THIS "AGENDA OF EIGHT"

I believe that true leadership occurs when diverse peoples can put aside their egos, personal agendas, and past angers and unite to support the common good of all Americans. But today, we see many congressional votes taking place along strict party lines. Our president is chosen through a system that is designed more to honor "good party-players" than great moral leaders who are truly concerned for our nation's welfare.

In light of the national trauma this nation has experienced as a result of the moral leadership crisis, I believe that for the first election of this new millennium, the leaders of both parties should unite in support of an agenda of restoring our country to the principles that built America from its founding greatness. I believe our political leaders need to remove their political egos and say they want to start this new millennium by showing the people they can unite and cooperatively support a group of leaders who support this Agenda of Eight—leaders whose lives fulfill the founding principles of this nation. The upcoming election can show that Americans can unite to face national needs, and we will be stronger for doing so.

Just as there were those who united to support our first president, George Washington, and just as there were leaders from both parties who sought out and supported Hoover for president, Americans today need to see that the current political parties can unite in times of need. In putting aside their political differences, our current political leaders have a unique opportunity to show Americans they can unite under a new declaration of independence from political squabbling. We are a great nation of great people. Let's show the world that this greatness still exists and that people of character can always set aside their differences to achieve important common goals.

Based on what we have shown about America's history, it appears to me that America does not need a great politician to become this country's first president of the new millennium. We do not need a person of wealth or of great public prestige. What we need is a person who has a vision—one with personal leadership skills, personal integrity, and high moral standards and judgment. We need someone who is following a clearly stated agenda for working to rebuild a new America for the twenty-first century.

Let us pray that God will favor us with one more opportunity to have a person of moral integrity to lead us into the twenty-first century as a united nation that will reaffirm America's founding principles.

3. REESTABLISH THE CONCEPTS OF OUR NATIONAL HERITAGE AND HISTORY BY CREATING AN APPROVED CORE CURRICULUM FOR OUR AMERICAN EDUCATION SYSTEM

In the course of researching this book, it has become increasingly obvious that a number of key principles and important stories of our nation's great heritage have been removed from the history books used in local schools. I could not find in the textbooks I surveyed, any of the stories related in this book. The countless examples of heroic and selfless events of our founding fathers had been eliminated or minimized. But I believe that heritage builds identity.

By sharing our nation's heritage through stories, we help to give a sense of identity and belonging to the next generation. We have allowed this heritage to be stripped from at least two generations. In part, it is this heritage and the resultant values that help us build our self-worth. Therefore, it comes as no surprise to me that, in nearly twenty years of counseling, the most common malady I encountered among people of all ages was a feeling of inadequacy— a dangerous lack of purpose and self-worth. We need to help America's young and old relearn that they have a great heritage and that they partake of that greatness as they reaffirm those values in their lives.

I believe that we need a counsel of wise and honorable Americans to establish a nationally required curriculum based on fundamental and accurate accounts of our country's founding stories that stress the basic principles that made America great. Like most of the other Agenda items, this one will require that we elect representatives of proven moral character who are in agreement with this Agenda.

4. ESTABLISH A "CARE UMBRELLA" FOR ALL TAX-PAYING AMERICANS

America needs to establish the following three items for every tax-paying American:

- A retirement system that will not be robbed from, and pilfered by, the political whims of the government.

- A method by which every American can have portable health insurance that will not be solely dependent on the contributions of their employers. As

American corporations continue the process of merging, consolidating, and in some instances downsizing, to remain strong and competitive in a global economy, their faithful employees should not get caught without proper health care.

- A tool that can be used in certain specified needs of life to assure that all Americans can afford their own home and a higher education, if they choose to pursue them.

I believe that by using the trust-note program I described in chapter 11, these three gifts can be given by our government to all tax-paying Americans. As this trust-note program is implemented, there are many side-benefits that could be built into the plan. Let me give a description.

Chapter 11 described how the trust-note program could replace the Social Security system for the next generations of Americans. By making this a system free from the government's ability to borrow from it, re-appropriate funds generated by investing it, or in any way divert these funds for governmental expenses, tax-paying Americans will have funds growing that can meet their anticipated retirement needs. My projections show that, at retirement age, just the monthly interest payments on this growing fund would exceed the current payments made by Social Security. Once the national debt is paid off, as described in limited form in chapter 11, this system may well need a course correction to meet the changing needs of those Americans who would own their personal trust note programs. Perhaps this restructuring could be a test of a national referendum vote on researched proposals.

I have now mentioned on several occasions that the economic and financial proposals I make in this book should relate to *tax-paying* Americans. Let me now divert to explain this reference. I believe that many Americans have been robbed of their self-worth and personal motivation by the current, well-meaning, nationally funded welfare and assistance programs. I also believe that many of those Americans want to work but feel financially pressured to stay on help programs because they do not see how they can make it without government assistance. Helping them realize the enormous benefits of becoming, and remaining, a tax-paying citizen can go a long way toward restoring their motivation and self-worth.

If the trust-note system were instituted, there would be a potential for developing a financial asset that could make every tax-paying citizen the equivalent of an asset millionaire. Since this system requires steady personal investments through payroll-deducted taxes, this benefit can, and should, be shared by those who are, and have been contributing, in proportion to the level of investments that they are lawfully making, I believe this incentive could help motivate people to want to pay taxes. Wouldn't it be a switch to see the IRS's role change from one of hunting down Americans who do not pay their fair share of taxes, to a role of verifying that Americans are tax-paying citizens? Let me give a quick summary of the main pieces of this trust-note program.

I. The federal government would write and give a trust
    note to every tax-paying American in an amount as
    determined below:
    A. The recipient's age at the time of the gift of the
        note.
    B. The recipient's taxable income over the prior seven
        years. (Having been a tax-paying American citizen

for at least seven years prior would be a requirement for participating in the program.)

C. This trust note would replace any future government-sponsored or government-funded retirement plans.

II. This fund would be held by a trust administrator for the sole purpose of being invested, so as to provide the following benefits to the note holder:

A. A long-term investment plan as allowed by enacting a law that would provide for the guaranteed retirement income of the trust-note holder.

B. A plan for portable medical health insurance for the trust-note holder and his designated family.

C. An investment tool that, as allowed by the enacted law, could be used to guarantee certain student- and home-loan programs (to be discussed later in this chapter).

The second point in this section is a method by which every American can have portable health insurance that will not be solely dependent on the contributions of the employer. We regularly see examples of American corporations going through acquisitions and mergers. Sometimes these dealings cause employees a loss of their sense of employment security.

In the course of today's merger mania, there is an unfortunate reality that those most often hurt are the faithful, tax-paying employees of merging companies. The company for which I work at the time of this writing, has gone through three such merger acquisitions, which has caused much anxiety for many of the company's employees. Perhaps the most commonly expressed fear was the specter of losing their health and retirement benefits.

My calculations have led me to believe that this proposed trust-note program could reasonably include a system by which a small portion of the investment income
could be used to help level out the fluctuations of hospitalization insurance premiums as employees get older. This
method would create a more certain source for funding the
premiums, which will make this system attractive and affordable for companies providing the insurance.

While American workers and their employers would
be able to pay the same amount into the trust-note program that they now are paying into the Social Security system, they also could pay the same amounts (or possibly
even less) into the program that they are presently paying
for their hospitalization insurance plans. The process of
administering this plan could be set up so that Americans
would be free to choose for themselves the type of health
care they want.

The system might work something like this: Once an
employee chooses his health care provider, the appropriate
forms would be sent to the trust-note program to authorize
payment to the health insurance provider to set up necessary deductions from the insured's payroll and to bill the
appropriate amount to the insured's employer.

Friends in the medical and the insurance industries
have assured me that employers as well as employees
would profit by having a greater choice of benefits. They
could choose higher or lower deductibles. They could
choose whether to have maternity coverage. It would be a
program of private choice, not government mandate, such
as in socialized medicine.

Because citizens would choose different plans and make
lifestyle choices about how much the plan would pay on
their behalf, there could be a possible additional invest-

ment incentive for Americans to reduce medical costs, so as to reduce the insurance costs paid from their personal trust note. An example of this would be that Americans who make fewer visits to the doctor would not be penalized with higher premiums. However, those who prefer to be less careful about their frequency of doctor visits would pay higher premiums.

Additionally, employees who change jobs could continue to receive hospitalization insurance coverage by paying the required premium amounts, as described by the plan administrator, into the trust note. This amount could be at a much-reduced rate when compared to the present system in which many employees pay their portion and the employer's portion when they are out of work (often referred to as COBRA plans). An allowance could be made for a portion of the investment income of the trust note, to pay the difference for a specified period of time.

Regarding the third item above, the trust-note program can become a tool to provide loans, which would be partially guaranteed by the assets that are continuing to grow in the individual's trust note fund. A system could be developed by which young Americans can borrow up to a certain multiple of the balance in their trust-note account. Every American (depending on age and level of income) would receive an initial amount in the fund from the government as their beginning gift. Because this balance would continue to grow with time, and as they continue to work and contribute into their fund, the asset base on which a loan could be granted by a financial institution also would grow.

Students could pay a lower interest rate on funds they need to borrow. (This could happen, in part, because they would be borrowing a portion of the funds in their own accounts.) These students would be repaying themselves (at least partially). This could help to reduce delinquency and default rates on these guaranteed loans, while they invest in themselves (through education) and in America's future.

Without an opportunity for higher education, I believe that our nation and our youth would lose the chance to achieve the dreams and the inventive spirit that is the trademark of previous generations of Americans. We have had our Thomas Edisons, our Henry Fords, and even our Bill Gateses, as well as countless other Americans who have helped bring our nation, and even the world, new achievements and successes. We dare not rob future Americans of the opportunity to achieve their goals and dreams. With the trust-note program, higher education can become an achievable tool to assist every tax-paying American in achieving his or her dreams.

Although nearly everyone I have counseled over the years has expressed a desire to own his or her own home, this dream seems to be slipping further and further away for many. I believe that, similar to the student-loan concept, assistance for first-time home buyers could be provided through the trust-note program.

To explain why I believe Americans should have the opportunity of owning their own homes, let me include a quote from one of our great presidents, Abraham Lincoln: "A child is a person who is going to carry on what you have started. He is going to sit where you are sitting, and when you are gone, attend to those things which you think are important. You may adopt all the policies you please, but how they are carried out depends on him. He will assume control of your cities, states, and nations. He is going to move in and take over your churches, universities and corporations. . . . The fate of the country is in his hands."

I am concerned that if we fail to help these potential first-time home buyers, we might face a national tragedy. The current trauma to families, and especially to children, affected by housing uncertainties needs to stop. Let me share some statistics to help put this tragedy into perspective.

According to *The Indebted Society, Anatomy of an Ongoing Disaster*, by James Medoff and Andrew Harless: ". . . 38 million Americans live below the poverty line.[35] Childhood poverty in particular has reached shocking proportions: as of 1994, 22 percent of U.S. children—more than one out of five—lived below the poverty line. Between 1978 and 1994 the poverty rate among children rose by an average four-tenths of a percentage point per year."

These authors estimated that by the year 2020, nearly one-third of America's children would be living in poverty. We have to find a better way to deal with poverty in America and with providing home and shelter to American families. I'm confident that we must, and will, rise to the need of America's future generations. As I have described, the trust-note program can become a vehicle for helping to provide homes for our nation's working poor—if we Americans will support the concept with our votes.

Additionally, we will give a new sense of an ownership of our country and an interest in our nation's outcome. By owning a home, people can gain a sense of personal ownership and pride in their communities and in their country. In order to protect their investment in their homes, new American homeowners will want to become active in bettering their communities and in restoring America as a nation of all the people. This ownership principle helped many of our founding pioneers weather the storms of adversity. I believe it will serve well in doing the same for America's twenty-first-century pioneers.

I believe there is a strength and reinforcement of personal integrity and dignity for an American family who knows they have been able to acquire their own home. It's not unlike Jimmy Stewart's character in the holiday classic *It's a Wonderful Life*, who helped to make first-time home purchases available and affordable for his community. The trust-note program can be used at a certain stage of its financial maturity to help guarantee the loan and down payment on a tax-paying American family's first home, and it can help restore dignity and pride of self-worth to first-time homeowners.

I believe there is one other area that home ownership can help to reinforce. It can add a renewed purpose to the institution of united families. According to a 1988 study by the National Center for Health Statistics, published in the May 27, 1996, edition of the *Los Angeles Times*, children in single-parent families are more likely to drop out of high school, to become pregnant as teenagers, to abuse drugs, and to get into trouble with the law, than are children who live with both parents. Similarly, social scientist Nicholas Zill reported in 1993 that "Children of divorced parents are, regardless of economic circumstances, twice as likely as others to have poor relationships with their parents, drop out of high school and receive psychological help."[36]

That being the case, statistics do not paint a rosy picture for America's children (our future). The divorce rate among all Americans more than doubled between 1940 and 1994. More than four out of ten marriages end in divorce. Only 55 percent of adult Americans are married—a lower percentage than ever has been in America's history. *Seventy percent of all children born since 1980 will spend at least some of their childhood as part of a single-parent family.*

Perhaps the gift of home ownership can, in some small way, help build an environment that will support the commitment to stable marriages and the strengthening of American families. Strong families are the bedrock of American civilization. We can pass high-minded laws, preach righteous sermons, invoke the need for loving tolerance, and elect the best leaders, but if we don't practice what we preach—if we don't model strong moral character for our children in the most impressionable environment of all, the home—all our other efforts will be futile. As William Bennett wrote in his anthology titled *The Moral Compass*: "No duty is more important than the nurture and protection of children, and if parents do not teach honesty, perseverance, self-discipline, a desire for excellence, and a host of basic skills, it is exceedingly difficult for any of society's institutions to teach those things in the parents' place."

No one ever said married life is always easy; it isn't. Just ask anyone who is, or ever has been, married. *Every married couple has struggles.* And marriage struggles are not a new phenomenon. The difference now is that we have made divorce the quick-and-easy "solution" to our marriage struggles. I suppose it's only natural in our microwave-society. Everything must be fast. Every problem must have a quick resolution—regardless of the ramifications. But the resultant breakup of families has a vicious cycle effect. Children who grow up in broken homes are more likely to have their marriages end in divorce than are children who grow up in stable, two-parent homes. And we already saw the statistics that revealed the other devastating effects of divorce and single-parent homes.

We cannot change the past, but we can resolve to make the future bright and good for our children and their children. Please resolve to make America strong by making your family strong. Please resolve to make your family strong by making your marriage strong. You can start with this "Standers' Affirmation" as written by Rejoice Ministries, Inc.:

> "I am standing for the healing of my marriage! I will not give up, give in, give out or give over til that healing takes place. I made a vow, I said the words, I gave the pledge, I gave a ring, I took a ring, I gave myself, I trusted God, and said the words, and meant the words . . . in sickness and in health, in sorrow and in joy, for better or worse, for richer or poorer, in good times and in bad . . . so I am standing NOW, and I will not sit down, let down, slow down, calm down, fall down, look down or be down til the breakdown is torn down!"[37]

5. ESTABLISH NATIONAL POLICIES TO GAIN AND MAINTAIN FREEDOM FROM NATIONAL DEBT

We stated earlier that in 1986, when the national debt reached 2 trillion dollars, it could be visualized as thousand-dollar bills stacked one on top of the other—and they would have a height of about 135 miles. In addition, the current national debt, which is almost three times that amount, would now be a 400-mile-high skyscraper! As a citizen and a taxpayer, does that frighten you? It should! As America continues with business as usual, how long can this ever-increasing monolith sustain itself before it topples over and comes crashing down on all of us?

It is imperative that we heed the following suggestions of one of our founding fathers, Thomas Jefferson, in two quotes used earlier in this book: "I, however, place economy among the first and most important of republican virtues, and public debt as the greatest of the dangers to be feared."[38]

And: "I wish it were possible to obtain a single amendment to our Constitution. I would be willing to depend on that alone for the reduction of the administration of our government to the genuine principles of its constitution; I mean an additional article, taking from the federal government the power of borrowing."[39]

I believe America must establish a policy akin to the current drug policy in many of our nation's communities: zero tolerance. We must move to a time when we will no longer tolerate our government financing its existence and extravagances at the cost and burden of this national debt.

Whether through a Constitutional amendment, or other legislative and policy means, we must no longer tolerate runaway government spending policies. America's government, like every American household and business, must return to a policy of a zero tolerance of budget overruns (spending more than they take in taxes and revenue). We must stand behind a policy of a balanced budget and a quick elimination of the national debt and associated national liabilities, as explained earlier in this book. I believe instituting the policy of converting to a trust note program to replace Social Security for future generations of Americans will help accomplish this goal.

Let us unite our political power to let our nation's leaders know we will no longer tolerate policies that sustain and promote a growing national debt. If we do not take this stand within the next five years, the burden and effects of this national debt could produce a credit crunch that could cripple American small businesses and even our government.

6. PROMOTE THE SEVEN BASIC PRINCIPLES UPON WHICH AMERICA WAS FOUNDED

We have seen that America's greatness came about as a result of the basic moral commitments of its diverse people. Gradually, we have moved further and further from that foundation of moral goodness. If we refocus on those seven basic principles and commit ourselves to honor and abide by them, we will regain our national greatness. Moral values are the compass that can steer our lives through the quagmires of every storm of life.

Every American who chooses to run for office should be willing to publicly affirm his or her support for each of the seven basic founding moral principles found in earlier chapters of this book. Americans should hold them accountable to these principles, and those who won't adhere to them, should be told, through the power of the vote, that it's time they seek a vocation other than leading this great nation.

Let's reaffirm that twenty-first-century America will be led by fathers and mothers who are committed to upholding the moral principles that were held by those who founded this country—and who hold our leaders to those same standards. This will be the bedrock basis on which our next generation will find examples, role models, and moral heroes after whom they can model their lives. In conforming our personal lifestyles to these high moral values, each of us can play a part in renewing America's greatness.

> I sought for the greatness
> and genius of America
> in her commodious harbors
> and her ample rivers,
> and it was not there;
> in the fertile fields
> and boundless prairies,
> and it was not there;
> in her rich mines

and her vast world commerce,
and it was not there.
Not until I went
into the Churches of America
and heard her pulpits,
aflame with righteousness,
did I understand the secret
of her genius and power.
America is great
because she is good,
and if America ever ceases to be good,
America will cease to be great.

—*Alexis de Toqueville*

7. REESTABLISH A UNITED NATION WORKING FOR THE BENEFIT OF ALL AMERICANS

Regardless of our racial, ethnic, religious, philosophical, or political differences, most Americans have one important, commonly held value: our desire for our children to have the best future we can give them. We cannot provide a promising future for our children if we adults are all pulling in different directions. For our children's sake, can we agree to disagree on many issues but agree to work together for America's future?

Let me restate something I wrote earlier in this book: America will regain its glory, energy, and hope, one person at a time. America will regain this glory when it realizes that its greatness hinges on the greatness of each individual American. Unless each American is recognized and valued as unique, special, important, and of worth, America cannot be a great nation. In this kind of America, there is no place for hatred, bigotry, and racism. We must reaffirm that we are "One nation under God, indivisible, *with liberty and justice for all.*"

8. Reproduce the gift of American independence and moral freedom to the next millennium of Americans

Martin Luther King Jr., had a vision, a dream. Mr. King's dream was that he would one day see his four little children grow up in an America where they wouldn't be judged by the color of their skin but by "the content of their heart." I must confess, I too, have a dream.

My dream is of an America where all American children can be proud of their heritage. It's a dream in which those children can build and achieve their own dreams, unfettered by government naysayers who would steal their dreams through regulations aimed at preserving their own jobs. I see Americans of all backgrounds, races, and religions willing to stand arm in arm, setting aside their differences to preserve the ideals of American freedom. It's a vision of America restored to high standards in and through the lives of its people. Driven by moral principle, this nation will uphold the weak; desire justice above wealth; and above all, it will again become *one nation under God, indivisible, with liberty and justice for all.* It's a nation where all our grandchildren will stand side by side, and as America's flag passes by, will say, "My parents and grandparents made a difference. That's why I stand here free and with dignity today."

If this is your dream too, please join me and countless other Americans in reaffirming your declaration of independence. We all must make a difference—today. Please make the commitment as written in the concluding pages of this book. Let's give back to twenty-first-century Americans the gift of America's greatness.

It is my hope that after you have read this book, you will want to play a part in bringing about America's return to the goals and values of our founding fathers and the many other Americans who helped make America great. Please consider taking the following steps in this restoration process of proclaiming your new declaration of personal and national independence.

- Please fill in and return the commitment card in the back of this book. The information from the cards returned will be compiled and made available to our nationally elected officials to let them know that we Americans will no longer sit by without using the power of our votes to impact America's direction.
- Get friends involved. Feel free to make copies of the commitment card and get as many as possible to join you in supporting the Agenda of Eight. In addition, consider asking one of your friends to help hold you accountable to the Agenda of Eight.
- Consider buying several copies of this book and using them as gifts for friends and relatives. They will be gifts to help restore America's true purposes and values. Order from your local bookstore, or call 1-800-917-BOOK. A portion of the proceeds goes to the efforts to promote the principles espoused in this book.
- Realize that your written commitment to help restore America will make your name available to your congressional representatives, showing the numbers of Americans who support the principles and solutions set forth in this book.
- Register to vote. In a recent election, it appeared that less than 50 percent of Americans who could

have voted chose to vote. Please realize that a united vote can make a difference. Some statistics say that it would take less than 5 million votes to determine the outcome of a national election. An electorate united to support this Agenda of Eight would make a landslide difference in the upcoming election. *Please register to vote and vote in the next election.*

• Write and let me know about how you are active in your community to support needed change in America. Perhaps your example can be used to spur on others in a way that inspires them to have a similar impact in their communities. Remember, you count, and you can make a difference.

AMERICA'S SEVEN BASIC FOUNDING MORAL PRINCIPLES

1. Perform consistent hard work as a lifestyle.

2. Develop a thrifty lifestyle.

3. Develop a sober lifestyle—freedom from addictions.

4. Emphasize people's equality before God.

5. Practice the duty of doing good works.

6. Emphasize religious pluralism—all denominations are equally legitimate.

7. Maintain personal standards of morality.

AGENDA OF EIGHT

Eight Principles
of a New American
Declaration of Independence

1. Apolitical/nonparty-aligned election of federal government

2. Restore grassroots citizen control to American government

3. Establish a "care umbrella" for all tax-paying Americans

4. Reestablish the concepts of our national heritage and history to American education

5. Establish national policies to obtain and maintain a nation free of national debt

6. Promote the Seven Basic Moral Principles upon which America was founded

7. Reestablish a united nation working for the benefit of all its citizens

8. Regive the gift of American independence to the next millennia of Americans

ENDNOTES

1. "A quixotic drive to pay back the national debt: the deficit fades, a new political fad arrives," Ken Jenkins, Jr.,*U.S. News and World Report,* August 11, 1997, vol. 123, no. 6, p. 61 (1).
2. Ibid.
3. John Winthrop to Roger Williams, *The Gentle Radical: Roger Williams* by Cyclone Covey (MacMillan, New York, 1966) p. 142.
4. See the complete text of the Declaration of Independence, the Constitution, and the Bill of Rights in the appendices at the end of the book.
5. Samuel Hopkins, "A Dialogue, Concerning the Slavery of the Africans" (Norwich, CT. Judah P. Spooner, 1776), p. 30.
6. J. Edwin Orr, "The Role of Prayer in Spiritual Awakening" (Los Angeles: Oxford Association for Research and Revival), p. 1.
7. Lewis A. Drummond, *The Awakening That Must Come* (Nashville: Broadman Press, 1979), pp. 15–16.
8. "One of the great strengths of Christianity is that it is a faith based on facts, not separated from facts."
9. Deanna Duby.
10. Halcyon House.
11. Kathy Collins, "Children Are Not Chattel," *Free Inquiry*, a publication of CODESH (Council for Democratic and Secular Humanism), Fall 1987, p. 11.
12. John Smith, *The Generall Historie of Virginia, New England & The Summer Isles* (1907). Vol. 1, chp. 10, p. 174
13. "How America Can Make Brotherhood Work," *Reader's Digest*, Special 75th Anniversary Edition, pp. 96–101.
14. "Heroes for Today," *Reader's Digest*, April 1997, pp. 115–116.
15. Ibid., 159–160.

16. "These Teens Know How to Say No," Mona Charen, *Reader's Digest*, March 1997, pp. 125–128.
17. Historical Tables, *Budget of the United States Government, Fiscal Year 1998*, p. 262.
18. Milton and Rose Friedman, *Free to Choose* (New York: Harcourt Brace Jovanovich, 1980), pp. 4–5.
19. From Goebbels lead article in the weekly Nazi newspaper, *Das Reich*, November 16, 1941.
20. International Press Institute Assembly, London, May 27, 1965.
21. See http://www.pbs.org/wgbh/pages/frontline/president/guide/glossary.html
22. See http://www.pbs.org/wgbh/pages/frontline/shows/scandal/etc/ads.html
23. See http://www.pbs.org/wgbh/pages/frontline/shows/scandal/interviews/liberman.html
24. *The Detroit News*, August 1, 1995.
25. See http://www.citizen.org/congress/reform/refhome.html
26. See http://www.geocities.com/CapitolHill/9428/info.html
27. See http://www.govt-waste.org/
28. See http://www.uvote.com/PHIL.html
29. See http://capitoladvantage.com/demo/demo1_feat.html
30. See http://www.votenet.com/
31. Andrew A. Lipscomb, *The Writings of Thomas Jefferson*. vol. 15, p. 47.
32. Vice President Thomas Jefferson to John Taylor, November 26, 1798. *The Writings of Thomas Jefferson*, ed., Paul L. Ford. vol. 7, p. 310.
33. See http://www.federalbudget.com/
34. *Congressional Record*, January 19, 1998 (Senate) pp. S199–S201.
35. Published by Little, Brown & Co.
36. See http://www.calvarychapel.com/library/References/Social/DivorceStatistics.htm
37. See http://www.rejoiceministries.org/
38. Andrew A. Lipscomb, *The Writings of Thomas Jefferson*. vol. 15, p. 47.
39. Vice President Thomas Jefferson to John Taylor, November 26, 1798. *The Writings of Thomas Jefferson*, ed., Paul L. Ford. vol. 7, p. 310.

To order additional copies of

send $10.99 plus $3.95 shipping and handling to

Wayne Guinn
13211 SE 26th Street
Vancouver, WA 98683

My Personal 21st-Century
Declaration of Independence

As an American citizen I promise, with God as my helper, to register to vote and to vote for national leaders who will actively promote and live by the following:

AGENDA OF EIGHT

1. Apolitical/nonparty-aligned election of federal government
2. Restore grassroots citizen control to American government
3. Establish a "care umbrella" for all tax-paying Americans
4. Reestablish the concepts of our national heritage and history to American education
5. Establish national policies to obtain and maintain a nation free of national debt
6. Promote the Seven Basic Moral Principles upon which America was founded
7. Reestablish a united nation working for the benefit of all its citizens
8. Regive the gift of American independence to the next millennia of Americans

Signed this ____day of _____, this year of_____,

by (print name): _____.

Signature:_____

Accountability partner's name:_____

As an accountability partner, I will help hold my fellow American accountable to promises made above.

Please keep this copy in a prominent place to remind you of your committment. It would be good to add your family's pictures near this card to remind you who it is for!

Wayne Guinn
13211 SE 26th Street
Vancouver, WA 98683

My Personal 21st-Century
Declaration of Independence

As an American citizen I promise, with God as my helper,
to register to vote and to vote for national leaders who
will actively promote and live by the following:

AGENDA OF EIGHT

1. Apolitical/nonparty-aligned election of federal government
2. Restore grassroots citizen control to American government
3. Establish a "care umbrella" for all tax-paying Americans
4. Reestablish the concepts of our national heritage and history to American education
5. Establish national policies to obtain and maintain a nation free of national debt
6. Promote the Seven Basic Moral Principles upon which America was founded
7. Reestablish a united nation working for the benefit of all its citizens
8. Regive the gift of American independence to the next millennia of Americans

Signed this ____day of _____, this year of_____,

by (print name): _____.

Signature:_____

Accountability partner's name:_____

As an accountability partner, I will help hold my fellow
American accountable to promises made above.

*Please add postage and return to the address
preprinted on the reverse side of this perforated card.
May God richly bless you and yours!*

Wayne Guinn
13211 SE 26th Street
Vancouver, WA 98683